INSIDE THE WAR ROOM

INSIDE THE WAR ROOM

First Edition, 2021

ISBN 978-1-954891-12-8 (EB)
ISBN 978-1-954891-13-5 (PB)
ISBN 978-1-954891-14-2 (HC)

INSIDE THE WAR ROOM

25 Winning Strategies for Politics

Ma Trong Tham

Contents

Dedication

To my grandparents — Ma Tổng and Võ Thị Lan, and my parents — Trần Cường and Ma Thị Ngọc Sơn. I will always remember and cherish your unconditional love showered on me, for it shaped me and made me who I am today.

To my lovely wife — Trần Đình Mộng Nga and my children — Ma Mộng Nhi, Ma Thomas, Ma Lam Trinity, and Savannah Castel. You are the strength of my life, the courage that fuels my persistence, and the happiness that defines my life.

Acknowledgements

My heartfelt thanks to:

Bác Hoàng Dung, Bác Nhị Lang, Fr. Walter Watson, Dr. Nalini Mitra (Colorado School of Mines), Dr. Woolsey (Colorado School of Mines), and Dr. Mạnh Văn, whom I always greatly admire.

My dear friends - Nguyễn Trọng Sơn, Nguyễn Cao Trí and Adam Wolf, have encouraged, helped and supported my family during a time of great desperation.

I am grateful to Sarah, who checked and fortified my English.

Many thanks to all of you!

Ma Trong Tham

Introduction

Apart from being renowned philosophers and political strategists, Niccolò Machiavelli, Sun Tzu, and Miyamoto Musashi had one thing in common - they understood the idea of winning and doing so by any means necessary.

These three men in the prime of their lives wrote three books, each that have become the pinnacle for military strategy from old to present. However, one could not be more wrong to assume that the books' strategies are only limited for use during wartimes because they were written for warring medieval laws.

Life is a battlefield, and each day brings a new opponent for you to challenge. If you live on a battlefield, then each obstacle thrown at you becomes an enemy that you need to overcome. To overcome your enemy, you would need a warring strategy to ensure you win at all costs. Essentially, if you can break down the strategies written in each book, you can pick out enough points to create an effective winning strategy for life.

However, because we have a culture that expects us to treat everyone fairly, be democratic in our approach towards issues, cooperate with other people, and, importantly, fit into a standard, our approach towards fighting these wars may be somewhat limited. The few people who step out of the fold to do what they find necessary always pay a heavy price for it. For example, Machiavelli to date still has a reputation of being a devious, cunning, dishonest, deceitful, and unscrupulous person because of some of the strategies he advised in his book.

It was so bad that an adjective was created solely to describe the kind of person he was. However, he was a preacher of "the end justifies the means" in his book. In a way, if people around the world find something that resonates with them inside his books and use them to their advantage in real-life scenarios, maybe he is not so far from the truth.

Sometime within the 5th century, in what was known in China as the Age of Warring States, Sun Tzu rose to fame and power as the general of an army that won many wars using interesting methods. He then wrote *The Law of War* to hand down the wisdom and knowledge he had gained from his many battles. The strategies shared in the book have been employed in many famous battles and shaped events of history. Along the same vein, Miyamoto Musashi wrote *The Five Spheres* as a five-part letter to his students and followers to teach them summaries of his strategies for winning sword fights.

On the surface, these books look like a "how-to" material on martial arts and armed militia, but they are so much more than that. The essence of these books, which are still studied by millions of people worldwide, is to provide tips on how to have a competitive advantage in life. Beneath the surface, these books are a practical tool for enhancing competitive success.

The values of cooperation, harmony, and unity at the forefront of this positive culture we imbibe are instilled in us in both overt and subtle ways. You read about them in books that are supposed to teach you how to get ahead in life, see them play out in the political correctness that has saturated any public space - both physical and virtual, as well as in the somber exterior that people present to the public.

However, there is one thing that these books or the culture do not prepare you for - the ruthlessness of the ongoing war in the real world. The same can be said about politics. Before Machiavelli, politics was strictly governed by ethics, at least if not in practice but in theory. There was a clear distinction between tactics employed by the military and those employed by politicians - one had leeway for ruthlessness, and the other didn't.

In fact, tracing the history of this ancient history back to Aristotle, politics was grouped as a subset of ethics. Ethics was defined as the moral principles that govern a person's conduct or behavior. Politics was defined as the moral principles that people in organized communities or social groups hold.

Machiavelli was one of the first people to divest politics from the shackles of ethics with his book *The Prince,* which has then gone on to redefine what the word means. What stands out the most from Machiavelli's treatise to rulers is how looking at the world from a demoralized view opens up a different perspective for actions. You will also pick up this same from reading Sun Tzu's *The Law of War* and Miyamoto Musashi's *The Five Spheres* (although the last two were more military strategies than political).

This brings me back to the purpose of this book. This war that we have to fight in life exists on many fronts. The world has become even more ruthless and cutthroat, even in business, arts, and politics. The most obvious detractors we have to challenge are our rivals that stand in opposition. We challenge opponents that will not hesitate to do anything if it means getting an edge over you every day.

Even more troubling and perplexing than the battles we have to fight with your rivals are those you will have to fight with the people who appear to be in your corner. Those that will outwardly play at things that are in your best interests, those who are very charming, agreeable, and friendly on the outside, but behind the scenes are plotting against you and sabotaging your efforts to serve their own self-interests and agendas.

These are harder to spot than your outright enemies and the most capable of creating destruction. They play subtle mind games of passive aggression. They use every secret weapon within their arsenal to weaken you from within, including guilt-tripping, manipulation, and offering help that never comes. On the surface, it looks like you have found your community to support your dreams but just below it, is every person for themselves - each tearing at the other to be the one to enjoy the results of it all.

While our culture will have us pretend or deny this reality by promoting a calmer picture of gentility, it would be foolish of you to make the same mistake. Human beings are base creatures governed by their self-interests. Any play at being a community will only last as long as that self-interest isn't threatened. So, you see, we cannot afford to live up to the ideals of selflessness, fairness, cooperation, and peace that society would have us.

If you do not look out for your self-interest first, someone else will find the opportunity you are missing and use it against you. It is either you strike first or be struck, eat or be eaten. Gone are the days of turning the other cheek in the hopes that your neighbor will extend you some goodwill not to repeat the same offense. If you turn your other cheek to someone who slaps you, rest assured that they will do it again.

What we need is not the seduction of peace, selflessness, and cooperation that human beings will never attain. That is just idealistic nonsense that gets nothing done. However, the blatant, if somewhat painful, realism and unrestrained truth that these men preached about in their books because they offer practical insight, knowledge, and strategies for dealing with the daily conflict and battles we have to fight.

Strategy is a way of life. It is the art of acting the right way even while under pressure to combat the most difficult situations. It involves developing ideas and thoughts that can modify already existing principles to fit life's ever-changing situations and apply that knowledge to real-life scenarios.

When handled properly, one can even say that conflict is a great tool for solving problems and reconciling differences. As the case may be, the amount of success or failure that you have in your pursuits can be linked to how well you handle the inevitable conflicts that you will face. As expected, our culture only prepares us to be reactive towards conflict and not proactive. When faced with situations we cannot handle, we lash out in emotion or try to avoid them. In the long run, all of these solutions are counterproductive because you cannot control the outcome of events, and often, they end up making things worse.

Strategy is about controlled planning. You already have an idea of what your end goal is. All that is left are the strategic steps that will bring you to that desired end. Strategic warriors are proactive, not reactive. They plan ahead towards their end goals, determine what fights are worth fighting and which are inevitable, and more importantly, know how to control and master their emotions so that it doesn't get in the way of their goals.

If they have to fight for their goals or defend themselves from threats, they do so indirectly and with subtle moves that make their machinations hard to trace. That way, they maintain the peaceful exterior that society, and politics at large, seems to love.

The idea of controlled fighting in political settings comes from organized warfare, such as those described in *The Five Spheres* and *The Law of War*, where the art of strategy was created and refined. Before then, war was a brutal, senseless machine for violence with no strategic ending. Humans formed clans and tribes that fought both with each other and within themselves in a brutal, ritualistic kind of violence for individuals to assert their dominance or heroism. However, as these clans and tribes began to evolve and grow more into cities and states, it became clearer that war came at a great expense. They could no longer afford to fight blindly as it led to self-destruction, exhaustion, and loss - even for the winner. The need for controlled and rational wars arose, and human beings have adapted to creating strategic moves that will have the least cost.

To that effect, I have compiled 25 strategies that everyone interested in politics should have in their arsenal - all taken from the strategies these three authors listed in their above-named books. Please note that the idea behind this book is not to teach or educate you on how to outsmart your opponents but to share the strategies that these men have already created.

Also, the knowledge shared in this book is not about getting anything you want forcefully or defending yourself against perceived threats. Rather it is knowledge about how to be more strategic and rational in your political moves when it comes to handling conflicts, managing people, dealing with opposition, and using your natural impulses to your favor instead of repressing them.

Suppose there is an ideal image you need to create for yourself. In that case, it should be one that shows you as a strategic warrior that manages difficult people and situations very deftly and intelligently, rather than an impulsive person that just reaches for the things they want without planning for the possible repercussions.

Part One

Offensive Strategy

Chapter One

Planning To Do Battle

"War tactics should follow the principle of deception." - Sun Tzu.

The most important aspect of any battle you will have to fight in war is creating a plan. Without a proper plan, all your aspirations could unravel in the blink of an eye. You can only go so far by being good or being capable. If you lack a proper plan of action to win or bring the results that you desire, you may end up losing out to someone less capable but with an airtight plan.

The same thing is applicable in politics. Each election, we hear complaints and arguments about seemingly capable people losing out to their less desirable counterparts because they didn't prepare properly for the race. It is easy to lose sight of what's important, and that is where a concrete plan comes into place - to act as a guide to bring you back on track when you begin to lose focus.

The key to staying one step ahead of the game is adequate preparation and proactiveness. Before you can test whether or not you can put out fires, you have to first make sure that you are fireproof. Proper planning will also make sure that you are not wasting your time on things that won't yield or contribute to the results you desire.

One has to be careful with how they invest their time, or you will find yourself spread too thin to focus on the important things. According to Sun Tzu, a winning army first ensures victorious planning before engaging in battle, while a defeated army is one that fights first before victory is sure.

A strategic plan brings razor-sharp focus and clarity, which ensures that its execution is effective and efficient. With a strategic plan, everyone knows what the end goal is, what roles they play, the outcome of their different roles, and what to fall back on when they experience difficulty. That way, resources, times, and actions do not go to waste.

That is what Sun Tzu means by saying that a winning team first creates a winning plan to assure their victory before taking the first step, while a losing team will first venture head-first into an enterprise before scrambling to create a plan to match whatever situation they find. Obviously, you can already tell who is more prepared to win between the two. If all your resources, energy, time, and allies are not channeled in the same direction, you end up going in circles, chasing after your own tails, and frustrating everyone in the process.

"In the aspiration of victory, there are five important key elements to observe:

1. *Know when to fight and when not if it's going to lead to victory or not.*

2. *Know how to use more troops.*

3. *Having the same goal and spirit in all ranks will lead to victory.*

4. *A prepared army will always achieve victory over an unprepared enemy.*

5. *A talented general who is not restrained by the king will be victorious in battle." - Sun Tzu.*

To rewrite this in terms of politics, what Sun Tzu was saying in essence was:

1. Choose your battles well. Know when to fight and when to cut your loss and regroup. If you are setting goals for your political career, they must be realistic and attainable. There is no point in reaching for something that you know that you cannot achieve. Instead, focus your attention on goals that are attainable and assure you of victory.

2. Know when to bring in more people to your team. You have limitations and blind spots that other people can cover. Learn how to delegate responsibilities to people who are well-suited or have expertise in them.

3. Clearly communicate your goals and objectives to everyone on your team so that you are all on the same page. Also, develop a system to better coordinate all internal activities. A united team with the same goals and mindset is already assured of success.

4. Preparation will always put you one step ahead of all your opponents and the game of politics. When you have made provision for all the steps you plan to take and created alternatives for when those don't work out, you can easily adjust to situations without losing momentum.

5. Micro-management can upset the balance of things. Once you have gathered experts on your team, give them free rein to do the job assigned to them without micromanaging every step.

Before you fight, you must first know your strength so you can properly compare yourself and your team to your opponent's. That way, you can easily determine if it is worth fighting before you begin.

These five points will help to understand where your strengths and weaknesses lie so you can plan properly towards your strategy.

"War has five determinants that we must plan. We must understand their correlations. One is righteousness. Two is the atmosphere. Three is the terrain. Four is the general. Five is martial law." - Sun Tzu.

Righteousness, in this case, is the cause that you are fighting for as a politician. It is the mandate that the people can get behind and give all support. Righteousness is the unifying factor that makes people rally behind you to be the one to represent them.

The atmosphere is the season and time. If you wanted to be literal, it could mean just that - the four seasons (whether hot or cold), time (whether night or day). But if you wanted it to be more of a metaphor, it could mean the situation of things on the ground. What is the general temperament that the people have? Are they happy or sad? Do they think it is time or change? How do they feel towards you? Warm and affectionate, cold and scornful, lukewarm and indifferent?

Like the atmosphere, if you wanted to be literal about the meaning of the terrain, it could be the topography of the area—high or low ground, smooth or rough roads, near or far distance.

However, metaphorically, it could signify your path towards your goals. What are your chances of winning? Do you have a smooth way towards it, or are there many bumps that you would have to maneuver? How far would you have to go to reach your goals? Do you have a high ground to stand on, or are you the underdog?

The general, in this case, is yourself. A great leader is one that leads by example and inspires others with their actions. Can people count on you? Does your leadership inspire people to throw their lot in with you? Do you exude confidence in your dreams? Are you strategic, focused, strict, courageous, and, importantly, kind?

Finally, martial law signifies the pooling and organization of your resources, including mental and physical manpower, funding and finances, weapons, and tools, as these will be your weapons. Basically, martial law is putting together and managing everything you would need to ensure your victory.

Anyone serious about politics must know all five points listed above and how to interpret them. If you know, then you will win, but if you do not consider them, then you are on the path to failure.

To that effect, Sun Tzu says that you must compare the following situations based on the definitions above to determine which team would lose and which will win, and in turn, determine if it is still worth fighting.

1. Who has the more righteous cause?

2. Who is the most skilled or talented general?

3. Who stands to benefit more from the current atmosphere and terrain?

4. Who follows martial law?

5. Who has the most sophisticated weapons in their arsenal?

6. Who meets their team more frequently to improve on their game plan?

7. Who has the fairest methods for reward and punishment to ensure the cooperation and loyalty of their team?

The answers to these questions will tell you who is more prepared to fail or win. When using the answers to these questions to plan for advantage, you must also take advantage of solutions that are beyond the expected line of action. The best-laid plans have been improved on to firmly but flexibly reflect and grasp the situation of things.

Sun Tzu insists that your tactics should always be unexpected to leave your opponents unprepared to counter. If you have the power to challenge them, pretend to be weak, so they become arrogant and careless. If you want to hit them very close to where it would hurt, misdirect them by acting like your target is far away from what they think is important. If you want to get close to them, then act like you are retreating, and they will lower their guard, leaving themselves wide open for your attacks. When they are disorganized, find a weak spot and attack. If your opponent is guarded on all ends, then be prepared for them. If they are strong enough to go head-to-head against you, evade them. If they are temperamental, harass them until they lose their temper and make mistakes due to their hotheadedness. If their camp is united, divide and conquer. If they are at rest and enjoying peace, cause unrest and unsettle them. Attack when they are not prepared and appear where they least expect it.

Let surprise and deception be the key to unraveling your opponent. They must never be able to predict your next move, or they will be prepared to counteract. Be like the magician that uses sleight of hand to misdirect his audience - while their eyes are distracted following the fake trail you give them, let your actions wreak damage in their camp.

These are the basic strategies towards creating a plan that assures you victory over your opponent. Before you make any move, you must first create a concrete plan that assures you of complete victory. A sketchy plan will at best bring the occasional battle win, but in the big picture of the entire war, such a plan is bound to fail. Your degree of preparedness based on the analysis above will make it easy to determine if you will win or lose once you make your move.

Chapter Two

Winning Without Fighting

"The ultimate achievement is subduing the enemy without fighting." - Sun Tzu.

According to Chapter 3 of The Law of War, Sun Tzu found it prudent that the ultimate achievement of war was to subdue your enemy without fighting. In Sun Tzu's time, cities grew and became wealthy not from engaging in commerce but from warfare and statecraft. Soldiers waged wars and went on campaigns to capture other cities and take their loot. Political and military alliances were created and discarded as the need arose. Warfare and diplomacy were the crutches by which most cities stood on, and they deployed either to vie for more territory, wealth, and growth.

However, if there is one thing that we have learned from the history of the wars ever fought, warfare brings not only more wealth and loot but also waste and burdens. For instance, the two world wars had a devastating effect on countries all over the world, with millions of avoidable deaths and aftereffects that left much of Europe and Asia devastated. Even the apparent winners of these wars were not left unscathed, as many were left poorer and weaker than when the fighting first started. We can still see this play out in many of the other wars that have been fought since then and even before then.

War is an expensive business. It comes at a very high cost of lives, psychological and social well being, businesses, economies, and cities. Sun Tzu believed that when it came to taking on an opponent, winning without damaging them is better than ruining it because the ultimate goal of war is not to win every battle fought without considering the casualties.

When planning an offensive attack against your opponent, Sun Tzu advises thirteen things.

1. *In military maneuvering, the supreme art of war is to keep our nation intact as a superior policy; taking over an undamaged enemy nation is more appropriate than breaking it. Keeping our army whole is the best policy. Capturing all the enemy troops is better than killing them …*

Surely, it is better to win over a group of people united to your cause than one divided between you and your opponent. There is nothing profitable about winning over your opponent and having to deal with people that are hostile or frown against the actions used. This is why whatever methods you must apply in beating your opponent, ensure that you will still have the support of the people at the end.

2. *By applying this principle, we can understand that winning a hundred times in a hundred battles is not the ultimate achievement. The ultimate achievement is subduing the enemy without fighting."*

It is exhausting to constantly fight with your opponent, especially if you are fighting to win. Aside from ensuring that everyone in your camp is working towards a unified mission, you have to look out for your opponent's camp to counter every move they make. It is an exhausting, time-draining, and energy-consuming process that could demoralize your camp and affect your long-term goal. However, everyone enjoys it when you use methods that break down your opponent's resistance without unnecessary scheming and battles.

3. *Therefore, the highest form of war is having a broader strategy than the enemy, followed by breaking allies of the enemy, then*

defeating the enemy in battle. The lowest is to besiege the enemy's city.

Even more important than fighting your opponent at every turn is creating a broad strategy that thwarts their plans. The next best course of action is to divide and conquer by breaking down the allies and camp of your opponent. Then you can match them head-on on the battlefield and be assured of winning. However, the worst strategy to follow is attacking your opponent in their stronghold as this is their home advantage, and any mistake from your end could spell doom for your plans.

4. *Siege wars should only be waged if unavoidable. Siege time is very expensive. It takes up to three months to craft and prepare weapons to attack city walls. It takes another three months to build the mounds of construction around the enemy walls.*

You should only attack your opponent where they have the home advantage if it is unavoidable. Attacking your opponent from a well-defended front will take too much time and resources before you begin to see results. At that point, while distracted with trying to break down their defenses, you leave yourself and your team exposed to their counter-attacks.

5. *If the general is impatient, he will launch his men to the assault like swarming ants around the citadel so that our troops could lose one-third of the casualties while the town still remains untaken. These are the dangerous effects of a siege.*

Control your emotions. In politics, every rash decision that has altered the course of history has been the result of one uncontrollable emotion or the other. Anger, impatience, irritation, lust, greed, frustration - all of these are dangerous emotions to be the basis of your actions because they cloud your judgment. Remember that a strategic warrior is proactive, not reactive. Acting based on your emotions is many things but proactive. Rash decisions will make you lose every advantage that you have already gained.

> 6. *Therefore, a skillful leader does not need to use the battlefield to subdue the enemy. He captures the enemy's city without having to attack.*

As said before, a skillful leader knows how to strategize to win the war without having to fight. A great leader out-strategizes, out-plans, out-classes, and out-maneuvers the opponent, such that when they see that they are out-matched, they are forced to concede defeat without fighting or suffer a humiliating defeat.

> 7. *He destroys enemy countries without putting his troops at great risk. All is to preserve the force by making use of strategy. Therefore, there is no wear and tear, and still, there is a great benefit. This is the strategy of offensive art.*

As said before, strategy is the key to winning without having to fight. Constant battles reduce the resources available to you and, as a result, reduces the number of wars you can wage on your opponents. If you, however, use very few resources when engaging your opponents by avoiding a fight, your team can defeat every opponent and the obstacles they throw at them with very little additional cost.

> 8. *When deploying the army and we discover that our soldiers are ten times larger than the enemy, then we encircle them. But if we are five times larger, we attack straight up. We divide our troops if we are twice as large.*

Keeping along with the theme of winning without having to fight, once you notice that you have outplayed, out-manned, and out-matched your opponent, force them to concede defeat and end the war. However, if you have a strong team but there are still a few loose ends to tie, go on the offensive before your opponent gets the opportunity to regroup. If you know you have enough resources, split them so that you can attack from multiple points at the same time.

9. *However, if the forces are equal, we make plans to defeat the enemy forces. In situations where the enemy soldiers are more than us, the best thing to do is to avoid direct attacks. If the enemy is too crowded, we retreat completely. So a small army should persevere rather than be defeated.*

However, if you and your opponent are equally matched, you can fight until the best-prepared team wins. If your team is outnumbered or out-resourced, then you must avoid direct attacks from the opponent. However, if you are completely out-matched, cut your losses and restrategize. The underdog should live to fight another day with a better plan than to display bravado and be completely destroyed and broken.

Chapter Three

Employing Subterfuge

"For what allows a leader and a general to attack decisively and successfully, where ordinary people fail, is foreknowledge." - Sun Tzu.

When challenging a formidable opponent, the surest way to ensure a decisive victory is foreknowledge. Throughout the course of history, wars have been won based on vital information that spies collected from the opponents. Political espionage began to gain popularity and spread during the middle ages.

Genghis Khan lived and breathed the teachings of Sun Tzu in the *Law of War.* He and his generals preserved the teachings in the book by practicing and improving on all the strategies Sun Tzu describes, reshaping the history of Asia and Europe in the process.

Genghis Khan was able to rule his Mongol Empire alongside Subutai, his primary military strategist, by employing subterfuge, including spying and scouting in advance for any signs of invasion from his enemies.

Before the Mongol invasion of Europe in the 13th century, Subutai spent a decade sending out scouts and spies to gather as much information as they could from the continent.

The spies were well trained to observe details about the enemy that could be important in conquering them including their military strengths and their defenses. They switched between three to five horses to cover large distances and maintain speed, ensuring that intelligence got back to their base faster than the enemy could account for or imagine.

Then, Khan and Subutai could make their assessments based on the information gathered. They made maps of the Roman roads, established trade routes, and made educated guesses on the ability of each city to withstand attack and resist capture. When they had gathered enough data to create a strategy, they attacked.

Foreknowledge allows you to forecast the likely behavior of your opponents. It shows you their weaknesses, their strengths, and their plans so that you can create yours to counter them. At the center of all strategic decisions is intelligence. Cold, hard information beats guesswork when creating plans.

Concerning using spies to gather intelligence, Sun Tzu had the following to say:

1. *Foreknowledge cannot be found by consulting with the divine being or by comparing similar situations. Nor could it be found by measuring the movements of heaven and earth.*

If we are factual, there is no divine being that will confer foreknowledge about your opponents to you, and you cannot make accurate strategies using conjectures and deductions alone. When making war strategies, you cannot rely on gut feeling alone. Lives are on the line and too precious to stake on a risky gamble.

In the middle of the American Revolution in 1776 at the Battle of Trenton, George Washington led his men in a surprise attack against a group of German mercenaries fighting for the British. After the battle ended and they rounded up the survivors and dead, they found an unopened letter written by a loyalist to warn of the coming attack in the pocket of the mercenary commander.

Here you can see the importance of foreknowledge play out. Had that letter been read, the mercenaries would have prepared a counterattack or avoided the attack rather than rushing in head first to their defeat. Making decisions based on wrong information or no information at all can have damning consequences.

2. *Foreknowledge can only be obtained from people who have accurate knowledge of the enemy's situation. In this respect, there are five types of spies that we can use: local spy, internal spy, counterspy, suicide spy, and reported spy. If we use all five types, no one can understand our scheme. It is a type of sacred organization and the greatest treasure of a wise ruler.*

In every political camp, there are different levels of people that have access to different classes of information. One level of information may not make any difference, but when you combine information from all the levels, it is enough to create a vivid picture for your strategy.

Recruit local spies from your opponent's locality and allow them to feed you information about your opponent's popularity among the people and the public actions they make. These are the easiest spies to make, especially if they already have an ax to grind with your opponent.

Cozy up to higher members of your opponent's political team and make them your internal spies to feed you vital insider information. You can convince them to spy for you with financial reward or fan the flames of malcontent they already have against your opponent.

One other thing you have to account for is that your opponents will have their spies in your camp just as you have yours in theirs. You can misdirect them by using their spies against them. Fish out the spies and use them as counterspies. However, be careful of using these double agents as they cannot be fully trusted and will double-cross you as soon as the need arises.

Another form of spying is using suicide spies, aptly named because they are dispensable. You deliberately feed them false information about your team to give your opponent. It involves openly doing certain things for the purpose of deception and allowing the spies to report what they have seen to your opponent.

Reported spies are the ones who focus on bringing enemy information to us. They may go deep undercover in the enemy camp and gather all the information you may find to bring down your opponent. For example, in 1976, the FBI planted Agent Joe Piston as a spy with the alias Donnie Brasco to infiltrate the mafia and acquire information that they would never have had access to. What was intended to be a 6-month operation extended into several years, and Joe was able to gather enough evidence to put away over 100 mafia members.

If you play your cards right, using espionage could be an effective way to soundly beat your opponent and ensure complete victory.

3. *So in the whole army, no one is closer to us than spies. No one is more rewarded than spying. No secret is more closely protected than the spy network. Spies must be used wisely and treated with kindness and virtue. We must use the utmost subtlety to ensure accurate reporting from spies. Subtlety is the key.*

Your spy network is a great resource for you and should be your well-guarded secret so as not to compromise them.

When handling your spies, treat them with kindness and benevolence but be straightforward and do not accept anything less than what you deem proper from them.

Remember that spies can bring down your camp with as much ease as they would your enemy. The same virtues that make them a perfect asset for your plans will make them the perfect weapons against your plans.

Apply utmost ingenuity and due diligence when sifting through the intelligence gathered by spies to ensure they don't pass on weak, incomplete, or false information. Verify information to ensure you have accurate information and that your spies are not working against you.

4. *Whether we want to destroy an army, attack a city, or assassinate someone, the first important thing is to determine the name of the commander-in-chief, trusted people, assistants, gatekeepers, and his bodyguards. We have to order the spy to find out this information.*

During the American Civil War, Elizabeth van Lew acted as a spy for the Union army. She freed all her slaves and used them to build a network of spies and informants behind the confederate lines. Nobody would have suspected such a seemingly unimportant woman of running a superior spy ring. The intelligence she gathered for the Union army was so good that General Ulysses S. Grant later attributed it to be a major reason they won the war.

On a political mission, do not overlook anyone - even the seemingly unimportant people - because they could have a role to play to the end of your mission. As a matter of fact, you stand a lot of intelligence to gain from people who are not seen or heard but hear much. These people can be convinced to help, or perhaps, not interfere in the way things play out. However, be careful with your dealings with them as they may also see or hear something from your camp that they will report elsewhere.

5. *When we discover the spy of the enemy who is watching us, we bribe them, take care of them wholeheartedly and release them freely. That way, we can use them as counterspies. Through these spies, we can recruit local spies and internal spies. Through them, our suicide spies will provide false reports to the enemy. And also, through them, our reported spies will be able to act as needed.*

If you have the good fortune of catching one of your enemy's spies, don't yet destroy them but look for a way to convert them to your side and make them counterspies. Intelligence gathered by counterspies can be instrumental toward creating a well-oiled spy machine. Through them, you know what people to use as internal and local spies, can pass false reports from your suicide spies, and collect information from your reported spies.

Chapter Four

Employing the Spirit of the Void

"Through emptiness, people naturally enter the right path." - Miyamoto Musashi.

A void is a place of emptiness - a barren wasteland where nothing exists - and as such, scares most people. People like to deal with predictable situations.

They want to know and be able to calculate the risks and rewards of a venture, so they can effectively plan. Going into a void is like losing your eyesight as you run into a tunnel or cave. You cannot see your front to advance or behind you to retreat, entirely at the mercy of whatever is at the other end. Most people would find that intolerable.

However, according to Sun Tzu, that is a very good strategy for offensive attacks in war - lure your enemy into a void, so they cannot see where your attacks will come from. He says:

> *Therefore, for those who are good at fighting, the enemy will not know where to defend. Those who are good at defending, the enemy won't know where to fight. Delicate instead! So subtle we can make ourselves invisible. Secret instead! So secretive that we can move without making a sound. That's why we keep the fate of the enemy in our palm. We attack, but the enemy cannot stop because we fight without people. We retreat, and the enemy can't follow because we escape quickly.*

The spirit of the void allows you to be secretive and subtle with your attacks while your opponents are scrambling to figure out what is going on and how to protect themselves. They cannot attack because they don't have a target, and retreating is out of the question because you are there, in the shadows, poking at all their weak sides. Their inability to attack, defend or retreat will do one of two things - tire them out or cause them to make a huge error they have no hope of recovering from.

When talking about how the warrior could employ the way of emptiness to their advantage, Miyamoto Musashi gave the following tips:

1. *The fifth is the Emptiness scroll. In this scroll, I talk about emptiness — that with no beginning or end, that with no depths or shallows, nothingness. This means that once you understand the principles of the Way, you'd have to let go of them.*

The emptiness scroll was the last of the five scrolls. Before then, he had talked about using all the four elements like the way of the warrior to your favor - earth, water, fire, and wind.

So it seemed counterproductive to make the last scroll a void that asked you to forget everything you had learned. But the first four scrolls gave the warrior almost rigid predictability that could be countered by any other opponent, especially one versed in the same skills as you.

2. *As a warrior, you'd become free and gain extraordinary strength. You'd understand the right rhythm for any moment and spontaneously attack and hit your opponent. This is the Way of Emptiness. Through emptiness, people naturally enter the right path.*

One of the reasons why he advised warriors to embrace the spirit of the void was so they could have an extraordinary advantage over their opponents. The void makes you flexible and free to attack and win your opponent without fear of retaliation.

In the 19th century, the business world was rocked by a mini-war between Jay Gould and Cornelius Vanderbilt called the Erie war. However, these business moguls were unmatched at the business war front because Jay Gould employed elusive means to goad the highly temperamental Cornelius into making several bad decisions after the other.

He created disorder in the markets that he could exploit to push out his competitor for the control of Erie Railway Company which managed the Erie Railroad. He would push his connections in the New York State legislature to create laws that would negatively affect Cornelius' businesses. According to American historian Gustavus Myers, members of the legislature would take money from both parties - one to support a bill and the other to oppose it. Jay Gould personally showed up at Albany with $500,000 that was rapidly shared among the members. On one occasion, an investigating committee disclosed that one senator accepted $75,000 from Cornelius and $100,000 from Jay Gould to vote towards a bill. He kept both sums and voted in favor of Jay Gould.

He would also plant anonymous articles in the paper that would smear Cornelius, but instead of looking away, his hot-headed opponent would take the bait and reply. In the process, he would give the article more publicity with his name attached to it, and Jay Gould's name would be free from all controversies. He kept Cornelius distracted like this with so many petty wars as a smokescreen so he wouldn't see what he was actually doing.

In 1866, Cornelius decided to buy a major part of Erie railroad stock. However, one of his board members, Daniel Drew, conspired with Jay Gould and James Fisk to sell spurious Erie railroad stock, thereby watering down the stock and reducing its value. In the end, Cornelius Vanderbilt lost over 7 million dollars to the scheme. After Jay Gould returned a large portion of the money to him under threat of litigation, Cornelius had to pass off the ownership of the stocks back to the trio that tried to swindle him. In the end, Gould won.

The strategy behind employing the spirit of the void is psychological. Once you know what exists, it helps you to infer what doesn't. The trick is to take away that knowledge of what exists, so your opponents are completely clueless about what doesn't. Once you have upset their strategic bearings, they become easy pickings for you and your team.

3. *In the world, if you see things the wrong way, you cannot understand things like "emptiness." We don't see it physically, but it is there in existence.*

As you work to understand your opponent, you must deny them the same advantage by making yourself as difficult to read and formless as you can. Since they will only be able to make conjectures and educated guesses, they will be easy to deceive. Be unpredictable. Throw them crumbs that lead nowhere, and they will not be able to defend themselves from you or counterattack.

Part Two

Defensive Strategy

Chapter Five

Build a Formidable Presence

"Anyone who fortifies his town well, and manages other concerns as outlined before, will never be attacked without caution. Humans are always averse to obviously difficult circumstances, and it will be seen as not easy to attack one who governs a town that is well fortified and a people that don't hate him." - Niccolò Machiavelli.

One of the best ways to defend yourself against an opponent is not to have them attacking you in the first place. Human beings would rather avoid difficult situations, so when sizing up their opponents and they find you powerful, they will think twice before making the first move. On the other hand, if they think you are weak, it gives them extra boldness to attack. Play on their natural inclination towards fear and anxiety to prevent them from testing you.

According to Machiavelli, here are some of the tricks involved in building a formidable presence, it deters enemies from attacking you first.

1. *German cities are completely free; they own very little of the surrounding countryside and only obey the king's orders when it suits them. They are not afraid of this or any possible power around them because they are fortified in such a way that everyone thinks that taking it by the direct attack would be tedious and difficult.*

The trick is to build a presence so formidable that your enemies will think twice before going against you. Create a reputation that gives you more power than you really have; let your opponents think that crossing you would be a suicidal effort. However, cement this reputation and make it more credible with a series of random ruthless acts. Make it random so that your opponent cannot peg the exact action that could set you off. That uncertainty works better as a subtle threat than any overt threat you could make. Unless your opponent is completely crazy or an absolute risk taker, they wouldn't want to start something when they are unsure of how you will react.

> 2. *This is because they have strong fortifications, with sufficient artillery and enough supplies in public warehouses to eat, drink, and fight for a year. In addition to this, in order to keep the people alive without wasting money, they always create jobs for the community with city-building works, and from this, the people are well-fed and supported. They value military training, and more than that, they enact many laws to support it.*

There are many people like that in life that will be stronger, richer, more resourceful, and more ruthless than anything you manage to build. Some of these people will be not only crafty but also unscrupulous, and any engagement with them will leave you on the losing end. There are like sharks circling around a prey - any sign of weakness or faltering is a signal to attack. The only way to deter them is by making yourself an unpalatable prey. You do this by creating a formidable reputation for yourself as someone who can go head-to-head with sharks and not lose.

One of the keys to creating a formidable presence is by giving the illusion of being well-prepared with enough resources at your disposal to independently counter any attack launched against you.

In 1474, King Louis XI, to the surprise of his courtiers in attendance, launched into an irate tirade against Galeazzo Maria Sforza, the Duke of Milan. Part of the surprise was because the king was usually unflappable, cool, and calculative, so his impassioned speech was out of character. Although the Duke's father was a friend, he claimed not to trust the son, accused the Duke of plotting against France to break the treaty between both countries, and threatened to. To the horror of everyone present, right in the middle of the speech, the Milanese ambassador to France, Cristoforo da Bollate, walked out. The king seemed to have forgotten about his presence at court.

His bold and irrational proclamation could create a diplomatic mess for France to clean up, so he invited the ambassador to his private rooms. While in the middle of a seemingly harmless discussion, the king began to feel out Bollate to find out what he had heard, and he confessed to having heard the whole speech and tried to convince the king that the Duke of Milan would never do any of the things he suspected him of. The king, in turn, told him that he had valid reasons to feel that way and would appreciate it if none of his words got back to Sforza. To make Bollate forget the whole experience, they tried to butter him up with the best accommodations and experience that France had to offer.

Of course, this was a ruse as the king had deliberately set out to give the Duke a subtle warning. He knew that Bollate would not hesitate to report everything he had said word-for-word, and he needed someone to pass on his threats without taking away from its severity.

You see, if the king had challenged Sforza directly, he would have fervently denied all allegations, and he wouldn't have been able to do anything about it. The same thing would have happened if he had taken a diplomatic approach with Bollate - they would have made the king and his wild suspicions appear crazy. So he had to warn the duke of what would happen if he continued down that path. It worked because the fear kept the duke in line for the next few years and made him the most pleasant ally to France.

From this story, we can pick out several things that the King did that were in line with building fortifications, as Machiavelli suggested.

1. Become unpredictable: The king was known to be cool and collected, which meant that his reactions were predictable. As a cool, collected person, it was expected that he would take the direct approach to make inquiries about the Duke's action, and they could have effectively managed him. However, his irrational outburst made Ludovico pause to consider if he knew the king at all.

2. Capitalize on people's natural instinct to avoid trouble: King Louis chose to send a message that made Ludovico think, rather than an overt one, this way, he could draw his own conclusions. Fear that comes from an open threat is not as powerful as the one that comes from talking yourself into it from a subtle one. When you coax your opponents into thinking they have unlocked a more sinister version of yourself, their imagination runs wild with it, especially if you don't give them hard, cold information to work with.

3. Turn the threat around: Sforza threatened to sabotage Milan's treaty with France, and King Louis retaliated by threatening to hurt him with something he valued. This move brought a new side to the king, and with a hint of ruthlessness that showed that Louis was not afraid of the Duke, he backed off.

The purpose of building a formidable presence is to prevent your opponent from attacking you. However, be careful with how you use this strategy, so you don't rile up the wrong person. This should only be used as an act of defense, not offense, and only when absolutely necessary. Constantly passing on threats may either throw down a challenge or make enemies out of the people you have pushed to the limit, which will undo everything you have worked hard for.

Chapter Six

Choose Your Battles Well

"To understand the situation, it is necessary to grasp and understand the conditions of the terrain and the condition of the enemy." - Miyamoto Musashi.

You cannot always rush in headlong into every battle your opponent calls. It is exhausting to the mind and body of the people who have to fight, not to mention draining the resources that could be better spent somewhere else. There is a limit to how much you can handle at the same time. There are only so far your skills, connections, and available resources will take you. Part of being a skilled strategist is recognizing where your limitations lie and where the strength of your opponent is.

You can always expect that it will end badly for anyone who overestimates their limits or underestimates the strength of their opponent. It is dangerous to allow some attractive promise of a prized conquest to trick you into overextending your limits, or it will leave you exhausted, vulnerable, and weak. Political war is expensive - even the victor incurs some hidden expenses. You lose time, energy, resources, political goodwill and instead gain an embittered enemy who will probably seek retribution.

Miyamoto understood that there would be times when you will have to navigate through tight spaces, and he had this to say about planning your journey:

1. *Through the course of one's life, there are many cases where you'd have to "cross the ford." When you are about to journey at sea, you need to know the location of the places you want to go, understand the capacity of a boat, and consider the weather carefully.*

Before you engage in any battle, you must first weigh the costs involved. Choose your battles carefully. Sometimes, it is prudent to wait or attack using more subtle means than a head-on attack. If you feel that you have too much to lose by going head-to-head with your opponent, abandon that line of action and look for one with more bearable consequences. If you cannot completely avoid the battle, ensure you fight on your own terms and not on your opponent's. That way, you can afford to choose methods that will cost you less.

Your strategies, in this case, should be the ones that stretch your opponent to their limits while affording you the flexibility to use your strengths. Make the cost of battle high for them and cheap for yourself, explore their weaknesses, and poke holes at them. With this method, you can outlast anyone no matter how formidable they appear.

2. *To understand the situation, it is necessary to grasp and understand the conditions of the terrain and the condition of the enemy. Understand if the conditions are floating or sinking, shallow or deep, strong or weak. By continuously practicing with the "measuring cord," the situation can be assessed on the spot. See and act at the right moment, and you would win, whether at the front or at the rear. This needs to be deeply considered.*

In 1558, when Queen Elizabeth I ascended the throne of England, she inherited a country that had been ravished. She set about creating a peaceful country and rebuilding the economy as she understood that England could not hope to compete against the other world powers like France and Spain at that point - not at war and certainly not by financial powers.

However, Philip II, the King of Spain, had other plans. He wanted to restore England to a Catholic country and fought against the Protestant rebels, determined to crush them. His short-term goal was to have Elizabeth assassinated and get her catholic half-sister, Mary Queen of Scots, to the throne, and if that failed, he planned to amass enough armies to invade England. Either way, war was looming on the horizon, and England was not ready.

Queen Elizabeth's advisors suggested sending an army to help the rebels push back at the Spanish, which would cause Philip to divert his attention and resources there and distract him from England. While Elizabeth agreed to send small troops to assist the rebels, she didn't agree to anything else. If she was going to fight Philip, she wanted to do it on her own terms and after weakening her opponent.

So she chose her battles well, defying her advisors and choosing to maintain peace with Spain by any means necessary. This move bought her enough time to gather resources to begin the creation of the British Navy. While maintaining the outward appearance of peace between the two nations, Elizabeth was secretly plotting to destroy Spain by exploiting their weakness - their finances.

She had studied the situation, understood the strengths and limits of her opponent, weighed the cost of doing battle, and chose a method that would bring the least consequences to her while dealing her opponent with the greatest damage possible.

3. *You should think of your body as the opponent. Whether you are dealing with someone who has retreated into a protected place, or a very large opponent, or someone who is well versed in strategy, you should think about the weakness in his mind. If you are not aware of the enemy's mind, you may mistake a weak person for a strong one, a person with no skills for one that is competent, and a small opponent for a dangerous one. The enemy may capitalize on this mistake. So become the opponent! You should analyze this carefully.*

One of the biggest contributors to Spain's wealth and economy at that time was the profit they made from their empire in the Americas. However, because it was so far away from Spain, they depended heavily on shipping. Philip had a large fleet of ships which he maintained with heavy loans from Italian banks, using the gold he shipped from the Americas to build credit with them. It was a weak system of operation. If anything were to happen to those ships, the Spanish economy would be sunk, literally.

Elizabeth understood this and exploited it by unleashing one of her captains, Sir Francis Drake, to act as an independent pirate, robbing the Spanish of their precious gold. With every shipment Philip lost, the interest rate on loan skyrocketed until the Italian bankers were increasing the rates not because he lost his ships but because of the threat of Sir Francis. Philip was supposed to unleash his army against England in 1582, but because of his money issues had to delay, buying Elizabeth more time to wreak havoc in the process.

Rather than making adjustments to his army according to his financial limitations, Philip decided to borrow more money to pump into it. He had been enticed by the promise of his prized conquest of England and by his holy crusade. On the other hand, Elizabeth used the little resources she had to build an impressive spy network to spy on Philip's every move and report back to her. That way, she knew how large Philip's army was and when he planned to attack, so she wouldn't waste what resources would be better used somewhere else, maintaining an army that wasn't ready to fight.

When Philip launched his army, he sent 128 ships full of soldiers on the way to England with a planned detour to pick up some of the soldiers fighting rebels. Elizabeth, already warned of their plans, sent a small fleet to disturb the progress of the Spanish. First, they sunk the Spanish supply ships, then when they docked at Calais to pick up their remaining soldiers, the English set fire to dozens of Spanish ships. These losses destabilized and demoralized the Spanish soldiers that they called off the invasion. In a bid to avoid further attacks, the

Spanish sailed north instead of south, planning to sail around Ireland and Scotland. The rough waters and weather dealt with what ships the English did not destroy in their attacks. By the time they got back to Spain, Philip had lost 44 ships, and the rest were not seaworthy either. He also lost two-thirds of his great army while England escaped with minimal damage.

Queen Elizabeth had successfully stretched King Philip to his limits while affording herself the flexibility to use her strengths. After weighing the cost of going head-to-head in battle with Philip, Elizabeth chose the path of least resistance - one that would bear little to no consequences to her and her country. In the end, the cost of fighting England became too high for Spain to bear, and Philip called off his crusade. That was how, even from a place of limitations, Queen Elizabeth I outlasted King Philip in battle.

Chapter Seven

Counterattack

"If you think there is going to be a deadlock, give up your intention immediately and use some other advantageous tactics to win." - Miyamoto Musashi.

The mistake that a lot of people make is thinking that there are only two positions to assume - attack and defense. A strategic warrior does not see battles in binaries, as there are many maneuvers that can be done in between that do not exactly classify as a complete attacking or defensive method. One of them is employing the method of a counterattack.

Whoever makes the first move and initiates an attack puts themself at great risk because you are showing your cards and telling your opponents what you planned. The way that battle progresses from there depends heavily on the way that your opponent decides to take your move and spin it. Rather than leaving yourself at the mercy of your opponent's strategy, why don't you become the player that has all the cards that could decide the game?

This strategy is particularly important when you and your opponent are almost equally matched or plan to use the same methods against each other. If you keep going at each other like that, the battle becomes unnecessarily drawn out because you are at a stalemate. To tip the odds in your favor and claim a resounding victory, Miyamoto Musashi suggests this:

1. *In large-scale strategy, if you sense a deadlock, that is, the spirit of "four hands," do not try to advance as that would make you lose many of your men. Quickly re-strategize and achieve victory using tactics that the enemy cannot think of. This is extremely important.*

Allow your opponents to make the first move. Let them show you the cards they plan to play so that you have more flexibility to counterattack. Just like you would a high-stakes poker game, call their bluff and bait them into making a mistake that takes all the power from their attack. Dangle the smell of victory in their noses and allow their eagerness to strike while you seem weak to throw them off balance or break them down.

2. *Similarly, in hand-to-hand combat, if you think you will fall into a "four-hand" stalemate, change your approach immediately. It is important that you improve the way you assess your opponent's attitude. Use a completely different tactic to win. You must be able to judge this.*

Being enslaved to your emotions will cause even the most fool-proof strategies to fail, and that's because emotions push you to make rash decisions that may upset the outcome of your plans. You can use your opponent's emotions against them and force them to make rash decisions. Hold back and wait for the right moment to turn your weakness into your gain.

If your opponent is an aggressive, temperamental person, bait them to lose their temper and act in anger. If they are impatient, use their eagerness to weaken them. If they are greedy, allow their greed to cloud their judgment. If they are overconfident, let it be the foreboding of their downfall. The best way to do that is to study your opponent and learn their behaviors.

Miyamoto did not just teach. He walked and lived his teachings too. One of the reasons he won his duels was because he never backed down from a fight. Rather, he found ways to adapt his strategy for each opponent he faced. He depended on the element of surprise to launch a counterattack against his opponents and took them down when they were unguarded.

In the thick of the Napoleonic wars in 1805, Napoleon was in one of the biggest binds of his military career. Both the Austrians and Russians had joined forces against him. In the south, a faction of the Austrian army attacked the French occupying Northern Italy, and in the east, another Austrian troop attacked, with a sizable Russian Army coming to join them in the east. The plan was for the Russians and Austrians to merge in the east and head towards France. The Germans, seeing that Napoleon's forces were stretched thin, were also considering joining the alliance.

Napoleon found himself boxed in by the machinations of his enemies. Any move towards fighting on any of his sides posed great danger for him, his troops, and France at large. It seemed like the only possible way out was for him to retreat with his army. Even his generals advised him to go take that route.

Meanwhile, the Austrian and Russian leaders were thrilled that they had Napoleon just where they wanted him. The Austrian emperor offered him a ceasefire, but in reality, it was a ruse by the Austrians to buy time to completely surround the French army. Anyone in Napoleon's position would have quickly swooped in on that deal - anyone except Napoleon because he was a formidable opponent who knew how to take risks. So it came as a shock to the Austrian Emperor and Russian Czar when he accepted to listen to their terms.

At first, they were suspicious, but Napoleon began to make erratic battle decisions that made it look like he was confused and afraid. The Czar sent an emissary that reported Napoleon's apparent agitation and distraughtness. The young Czar, chomping at the bit to get his first victory against Napoleon, could not allow this golden opportunity to waste, so he launched an attack.

However, because his decision was spurred by impatience and heightened excitement, the Czar rushed his troops to attack the break-in Napoleon's line. This move left his own center exposed to attacks. By the time his general noticed this mistake, it was too late to turn back. The tables turned, and Napoleon became the aggressor. Some French troops had arrived for reinforcement, and they attacked the Russians.

The best position to disguise an offensive attack is using a defensive maneuver. As I said before, war tactics do not have to be an either/or option. You do not always have to choose between an offensive or defensive strategy. In fact, you stand a risk of boxing yourself in using that method.

Being offensive as a rule of thumb creates more enemies and increases the risks of making costly decisions, while being defensive corners you into a position your opponent can exploit. Either way, your actions, and responses are predictable - remember that Miyamoto won most of his duels by using the element of surprise.

When it looks like you have been cornered and there's no way out, do not accept defeat just yet. You can turn almost any situation around if you learn to act like Napoleon - play weak to trick your opponent into making rash decisions from overconfidence, then catch them off guard by launching an unexpected counterattack. This way, what appeared to be your weakness becomes your strength.

Another person who was famous for using this method of baiting and switching was President Franklin Roosevelt.

He had a habit of retreating into himself and his opponents, thinking that it meant weakness, would go on a rampage trying to tarnish his name and attacking his methods. Each time, he would wait for them to exhaust all the negative things they had to say about him and would pick a strategic moment to use their words as ammo against them. It always worked.

On September 23, 1944, he made his famous Fala speech because his Republican opponent accused him of using the taxpayers' money to care for his Scottish Terrier, Fala. He said:

> *These Republican leaders have not been content with attacks on me, or my wife, or on my sons, that they now include my little dog, Fala. Unlike myself and my family, who don't resent these attacks, Fala does. Fala, being a Scottie, was furious to learn that the Republican fiction writers had concocted a story to say that I had left him behind on the Aleutian Islands and sent back a destroyer to find him at the expense of two, three, eight, or twenty million dollars to the taxpayers. He has not been the same dog since. While I am accustomed to hearing malicious untruths about myself, I think I have the right to resent and object to libelous statements about my dog.*

The speech was well-received by the audience to the eternal embarrassment of the republicans because he used their words as a counterattack against them. He allowed them to make the first move, exposing their strategies and blindspots. He used their aggression and impatience against them by goading them to speak rashly. In the end, that speech became instrumental towards his win in the elections because it endeared him to many people.

Your retreat should be a means to an end and not an end itself - the former is a strategy towards winning while the latter is a surrender in acceptance of defeat. Retreat with the mindset that it is temporary, and you may have to turn and fight back.

Chapter Eight

Retreat To Advance

"When we get to dangerous grounds first, we will be able to occupy high, sunny places where it will be easy for us to observe and wait for the enemy. If the enemy goes there first, we should not fight, and we should retreat." - Sun Tzu.

S ometimes, you will find yourself in a tight spot that makes victory over your opponent unattainable. When you have weighed the pros and cons of forging ahead and taking some space to regroup and the latter looks like the better option, do not be ashamed to retreat. Sun Tzu goes on to say:

1. *Don't move unless you see a clear advantage. Do not use soldiers unless there is something to gain. Do not fight if we are not in danger. The king cannot mobilize the army because of personal anger. The general cannot engage in battle because of personal outrage. Only mobilize the army if it is beneficial for the country, otherwise do not move.*

Another reason why a retreat might be the best course of action for you to follow is that you sometimes lose perspective of the war while in the thick of battle. Miyamoto Musashi defined perception thus:

2. *There are two ways to see - perception and sight. Perception means concentrating strongly on the opponent's mind and terrain of the battle place. It also involves observing the situation*

of the battle and seeing how the advantage changes. That is the way to win.

He goes on to say:

3. *In small- and large-scale strategies, there is no reason to gaze at minute things. As I mentioned before, if you focus closely on specifics, you would forget the big things. You would lose your perspective, and victory would elude you.*

You can get so sucked into the thrill of winning, the exchange of wit and parrying shots that you forget why you need to win or how you intend to win. Perception is very important in battle - once you lose sight of important things, you are well on your way to losing the battle already.

When you notice that you do not see things as clearly as you should, take a step back to regroup and detach yourself from influences that may be narrowing your sight.

Retreating in the face of impossibilities is not a sign of weakness but one of strength. We all love a good underdog story - the one who rose against all odds to gain complete victory over their opponents. However, out of the underdogs that made it, there are thousands more like them that failed before they got the chance to find their feet.

If your circumstance does not give you firm ground to plant your feet, do not risk everything you have on a gamble. There is a popular quote from Napoleon that goes:

4. *Strategy involves the use of both time and space. I am less concerned about the latter than the former. You can recover space but cannot recover lost time.*

Space in this sense is the battle area. The space where you battle should afford you an advantage over your opponent - you should be able to face them and attack with both long-range and short-range strikes. Time, on the other hand, is the window of opportunity you have to respond quickly and decisively to your opponent's attacks.

Revisiting Napoleon's quote, if you lose the space to battle an opponent because you cannot find any advantage in it for you, you can always find another space more suited for your needs for a rematch. However, if you miss the window of opportunity to respond swiftly to an attack or launch one, you may never get it back again.

Retreating affords you the luxury of sacrificing space for time. It does not mean you have completely given up, but if you choose not to fight, you are buying yourself time to find the perfect window of opportunity to act.

If your enemies mistake this for weakness, let them. If they advance, allow them and evade every attempt they make to draw you out. Remember, time is more valuable than space. Allow your perceived weakness to feed their arrogance or your perceived nonchalance to feed their aggression. Sooner, rather than later, they will make a mistake that will give you the perfect opening to act.

Time reveals all things and balances the scale, sometimes, without even any input from you. The summary of Murphy's law is that anything that can go wrong will go wrong. Buy yourself time until everything that can go wrong indeed goes wrong.

The Chinese have a concept called Wu Wei, which plays an important role in her statecraft and Taoism. Wu Wei simply means action through inaction. It describes knowing the reality of any situation, accepting it, and conserving your energy. In other words, it means taking control of your situation by not trying to control your situation.

When you try too hard to fight your circumstance, you could make things worse for yourself than it already is. Sometimes, the best course of action is to lay low and do nothing, and as Murphy's law states, anything that will happen will.

If your situation calls for you to retreat, but you fight against it by continuing to advance towards your opponent, you might think you are making progress, but the reality is that you are marching towards your doom.

When Frederick the Great ascended the throne in 1740, he could only be called the King *in* Prussia because his territories were scattered all over, and his kingdom was only a portion of Prussia. So he set about acquiring the rest of the kingdom so he could be called the King *of* Prussia.

However, there was one problem. Some of the territories he sought to reclaim were under the control of Habsburg, which was ruled by Maria Theresa of Austria. This led to several wars and hostilities between Prussia and Austria. After the first Silesian war, Frederick suspected that Maria Theresa would launch another attack to regain the city, so he formed an alliance with France and invaded Bohemia. At the same time, the Saxons joined Austria to push back at Frederick's army. However, his army claimed so many victories that Austria was forced to sign a treaty to hand over Silesia to Prussia and ensure peace.

Although the treaty was signed, Austria still remained in several wars until they signed another treaty in 1748. Less than a year after signing it, Maria Theresa was back to seeking an alliance with France and Russia to beat back Prussia. In 1756, in the bid to forestall England from financing a Russian army to Prussia's border, Frederick also gained an alliance with England.

So that when the Seven Years' War began between the British and the French in 1756, both Prussia and Austria had switched allies from the original ones they formed during their own wars. In the thick of war, Frederick found his army battling an alliance of enemies made up of Austrian, Russian, Swedish, Roman, and French troops, his only support being Great Britain and her allies, Brunswick, Hesse, and Hanover.

His situation became worse in 1761. After having gotten what they wanted from the Indian and American colonies, the British stopped their financial support for Prussia and left Frederick in quite a bind. Frederick, whose usual style of fighting was an aggressive, offensive attack, had to revert to defensive methods to protect himself. His new strategy involved maneuvers that would buy himself and his army enough time to slip through the net that his enemies had laid in wait for him. He did this dance of retreat for years, barely managing to avoid disaster and waiting for when he would have a window of opportunity to turn the tables around.

Fortunately for him, Murphy's Law happened, and the ruler of Russia, Czarina Elizabeth, died which led to the succession of her German nephew, Peter III. Peter was sympathetic to the Prussians and completely enamored of Frederick that he pulled Russia out from the war, returned the Prussian lands that Russia took, and offered his army to Prussia to fight against Austria.

This event became aptly known as the Second Miracle of the House of Brandenburg. Right at the point where he needed it, a window of opportunity landed on his laps that led to his success in the war. Had he rushed in headlong with fake bravado or completely surrendered, he would have lost more than he already had. Instead, he waited and didn't make his situation worse by fighting it.

By disengaging and retreating from your opponent, you do not run a loss in the long run. Instead, it buys you time to rethink your ideas, consider your circumstances, and shuffle things around. Time is your biggest ally - it settles things into place. When you sacrifice space for time, it buys you the power to act.

Part Three
Solo Warfare

Chapter Nine

Gaining Power Through Merit or Fortune

"One does not need genius or good fortune to attain civil power, but rather fortunate intelligence." - Niccolò Machiavelli.

There are two ways to gain power - you are either born into it, or you work into it. Like wealth, it is easier for people born into power to recreate it. They already have access to the right tools, know all the right people, and the right procedure to follow.

However, for the common person who was not born into power or was not raised in close proximity to it, it is an entirely different ball game. The journey from commoner to political elite is a long one with several challenges involved.

Machiavelli, when describing the ways by which an ordinary person can rise to power and hold on to it, had the following to say.

> 1. *Now it is clear that for an ordinary person to rise to the position of a prince either by his ability or luck, one of these will help to mitigate difficulties to an extent. However, those who depend on luck the least will come out stronger.*

According to Machiavelli, there are two ways by which an ordinary citizen can gain political power - through their abilities or through luck. Either one of these things can help to ease your way as you do your socio-political climb.

However, of the two who depend on luck and abilities, the one who depends on the latter will always thrive over the other. The reason is easy enough to infer. Luck is beyond your control. You cannot influence or manipulate it to always be in your favor. Relying on luck alone is like building a sandcastle and hoping the weather remains kind enough to leave your structure standing.

> 2. *Territories that rise too quickly, like all things in nature that are born and grow rapidly, cannot lay the proper foundations and groundwork fixed in such a way that the first storm does not destroy them.*

There are many things that you can control to make your construction last longer, such as the kind of material you use and where you build it, but you cannot control the weather. If you choose not to lay the right foundations, follow due process, or use the right materials, one day the weather will turn against you, and all your hard work will be for nothing - blown away by the wind, never to be recovered.

When you depend on luck to build your political career, it is not a matter of "*if*" it will but "*when*" it will. If you are not prepared to flow along with the changing tides, you will be left behind with only the ruins of your career to keep you company.

> 3. *Those who become princes from commoners through good fortune have little difficulty rising to the top but find it hard to remain on the throne. They experience no hardships on the way up because they fly, but once they get to the top, they have many. Such goes for people who acquire a state by buying it or by the favor of one who bestows it. The same thing also applies to rulers who, by the corruption of soldiers, came into power.*

When Machiavelli spoke of fortune, he meant luck, favor, goodwill, fate, chance, or opportunity. Fortune has so many advantages, especially for people starting out with no prior experience. It smoothes the way and makes the journey easier. You ride to the top faster without a hurdle in your way. However, one of the disadvantages is that it hardly prepares you for the real work you will face when you hit the top. That is why it is hard to find someone who got to the top solely by luck and maintained the position using that same means.

> 4. *Unless, as noted, those who suddenly become princes have great abilities that they know they have to be ready at once to hold on to what luck has given them. They must understand that they need to lay a solid foundation for their status, like others that had come before did.*

An example of one who rose to power through fortune is Cesare Borgia, the illegitimate son of Pope Alexander XI. Cesare was originally groomed to have a career in the church. By the time he was 15, he already became the Bishop of Pamplona, and with his father's elevation to Pope, he became a cardinal at 18.

His older brother, Giovanni, was the one originally groomed for political office, but he died in 1497, leaving the family hopes of having a political position to Cesare. In 1498, Cesare resigned from his cardinalate to join the military, and that same day, the French King, Louis XII, made him the Duke of Valentinois. Thus began Cesare's political ambition.

He got his first position as goodwill from the King due to his father's machinations and alliance with France. Pope Alexander, seeing an opportunity to push Cesare to an even better political position by carving out a state for him in Northern Italy, propositioned the King for Romagna and was granted it. However, Alexander's bid to uplift his son had many challenges.

The only territories he could give his son were those owned by the church. If he did that, he knew he would be opposed by the Venetians and the Duke of Milan. Also, the only army that could have helped was controlled by people who would not want the church to acquire more power. He decided that the best course of action was to disrupt the state of things, and while the powers that ruled Italy were scrambling in confusion, he could take what he wanted for Cesare. So, he brought King Louis to Italy and caused a disruption. When the King invaded Italy in 1499, and Ludovico Sforza had been ousted as the Duke of Milan, Cesare accompanied him to Milan.

However, this was where things began to turn sour for Cesare. King Louis appointed him as the commander of the papal armies, which were made up of Italian mercenaries, 300 cavalries, and the 4,000 Swiss infantry he sent.

Cesare began to suspect that his troops were not loyal to him, and he couldn't do anything about it because they had the support of the King. He was also afraid that the Orsini mercenaries he used would betray him. He tried to acquire more territories, but the King stopped him from attacking Tuscany. At that point, he knew that he couldn't trust any of these people and decided to rely only on the goodwill and armed forces of other people for his plans.

Cesare brought in good policies that improved the lives of the people in the regions he ruled. Therefore, it was hard for his enemies to remove him from power, but it didn't stop them from plotting. Understanding how tenuous his situation was because everything he had, he could only keep on the goodwill of the Pope, Cesare decided to do four things before his father passed.

1. He had to kill all the families of all the lords he defeated so they would not come back to seek revenge or a claim to his territories.

2. He had to gain the loyalty of all the powers in Rome so that they would support him, not the new Pope when his father died.

3. He would gain the support of the College of Cardinals.

4. He would have gained so much power and stability that he could push back the first wave of attacks when his father eventually died.

He had already worked his way through the first three items on the list and was on the fourth one by trying to invade Tuscany when his father suddenly died. When Alexander died, Romagna was the only city held by Cesare that was settled. He only had a tentative hold on every other place.

The new Pope, Pope Pius III, supported Cesare, and for a while, it seemed like all was well. Unfortunately, after only twenty-six days in the papacy, he died. His successor, Pope Julius II, was an old enemy of Cesare's that tricked him into supporting his papal ambition by offering him money and continued papal backing for his ambitions. After Pope Julius won by unanimous decision, he promptly disregarded his promises. Upon realizing his mistake, Cesare tried to remove Julius from the papal seat, but he failed at every turn. Having lost the goodwill of the only thing keeping his ambition together, Cesare quickly hurtled towards destruction.

5. *As stated above, any prince that does not lay his foundation may be able to do so after with outstanding talent, but with so much trouble and danger to the building.*

Although Cesare gained power through fortune, he tried to change the foundation of his power to his abilities and, in the process, hurt a lot of people that became his enemies. During the conversion, his position was made extra dangerous as a result of this. But the final nail that sealed his coffin was that he ran out of good fortune and everything he built came tumbling.

When talking about men who came into power by their own merit and abilities, Machiavelli had this to say:

6. *When considering their actions and lives, we can see that they do not owe anything they achieved to luck beyond the opportunity that gave them the material to mold into any shape that best suits them. Without that opportunity, their abilities would have*

been wasted, and without those abilities, the opportunity would have been in vain.

An example of an ordinary citizen that rose to power through his merit was President Andrew Jackson. Born to Irish immigrants, Andrew Jackson lived his early life in abject poverty and hardship. Different circumstances led to the death of every of his immediate family members until he was the only survivor. After a series of false starts, Andrew finally made headway with his life by becoming a wealthy Tennessee lawyer. In 1812, Andrew fought in the war between the United States and Britain. He earned national fame as a war hero through his leadership and conduct during the war. This reputation gave Andrew the opportunity to become one of the most influential political figures in American history, and he seized it.

In 1824, he contested against three other nominees for the presidency in one of the tightest presidential races in American history. All of these men were from different parts of America. However, of all of them, Andrew was the only non-elite - a simple worker from the other side of the tracks that worked his way up into affluence and influence. He won the majority of the popular votes, but since there was no majority winner in the Electoral College, the House of Representatives decided the winner of the election. One of the presidential hopefuls, John Quincy Adams used his political background to convince Clay into supporting his claim to the presidential title.

However, Andrew did not give up and contested in the next elections where he soundly defeated the incumbent, Adams, to become the seventh president of the United States. Andrew Jackson's merit as a military hero won him the presidency. His accomplishments during the war sparked pride in the voters who lovingly called him *Old Hickory and the Hero of New Orleans.* Apart from his achievements, he remained in the mind of the people as the leader who rose from nothing - an ordinary citizen.

7. *Those who, like these men, become princes from brave deeds acquire territories with difficulty, but they keep it with ease. The difficulties they face in acquiring it arises partly from the new rules and methods they are forced to enforce to establish their government and secure it. It is important to remember that there is nothing more difficult to solve and more dangerous than the adventure of creating a new regime. This is because the founder will meet enemies who have enjoyed many privileges under the old regime, and lukewarm supporters, in those who enjoy the new laws, will not actively protect the new collaborators.*

This fits Andrew's story to the last letter because, throughout his eight years in the office, he claimed to represent the interests of common white Americans, especially those from the South and West, over the country's powerful and wealthy elite. His proclamations did not endear him to the powers that were because they undermined all the privileges they were enjoying before he came into office. This later led him into a series of bitter political struggles to maintain his position.

Chapter Ten

Be Present

"As long as the prince resides there, it will be very difficult for others to take the throne." - Niccolò Machiavelli.

T he biggest mistake you could make is by imagining that after winning over your opponent, the war ends. Politics is a continuous war with different battles fought every day.

Before you gain office, your battle is with your opponent, but once you get the seat of power, your battle is against anything that will seek to take that power from you.

One of the hardest offices to take over is one that has different laws, agendas, customs, or languages from what you are used to. It can be hard to keep everyone together to ensure you all have a common goal. Machiavelli believes that the way to do this is to remain present.

1. *Managing acquired territories in countries with linguistic, custom, or legal differences is difficult and requires a bit of luck and a lot of effort. One way to work around this is if the prince decides to live in the territory to secure his position. While staying there, he can spot problems immediately and fix them. If he doesn't live in the territory, it might be easy to overlook problems until they become too severe to fix.*

As Machiavelli stated, being present in a new area you are governing allows your position to remain secure because you can easily spot problems before they escalate and take measures to curb them. It allows you the freedom to control, regulate, or repress whatever situations come up as you deem necessary.

Establishing your presence, especially as a politician that will have to deal with opposition from think tanks and political opponents or bureaucracy from committees and state departments will protect your administration from being tossed around by people, pushing different agendas or people with different goals and allegiances than your interests.

When you notice these situations do not align with your goals crop up, nip them in the bud to prevent them from blowing up all over your face. Your presence should not be irregular or off/on the thing. Be hands-on; let people feel your presence.

2. *Another benefit of having the prince reside in his acquired territory is that it prevents the officials from abusing his new subjects and the easy access keeps the people satisfied. The prince needs to give his subjects many reasons to love him while still maintaining their fear. Any foreign state that wants to attack this territory must also be very afraid. As long as the prince resides there, it will be very difficult for others to take the throne.*

Another reason why you should make your presence felt is to curb the excessive actions of your staff or cabinet against your constituents in your name. It will not end well for you if members of your team harass, mistreat, abuse, or hurt the people you are supposed to lead in your name. One of the ways that you can hold on to power is securing yourself in the mind of the people as having their best interests. As long as the people love you and as long as your presence serves them well, it will be hard for anyone else to try to take power from you.

However, it is understandable that with so many responsibilities, both national and international, you might not be physically present everywhere that you are needed. Since you cannot be in more than one place at the same time, being present in today's context would mean remaining informed on the daily progress of your political mandates and engaging your community. Every political leader has to be available when needed and be ready to show others how to follow. Failure to do this encourages behaviors that could spell doom for your political aspirations.

Some of the most promising politicians have had their careers affected because while playing the long game, they forgot to keep their eyes on the ball. It is easy to get carried away about the future. You have dreams to change the world, and you plan to begin with the office that you manage. However, your priority should be to effectively manage the present while making plans for the future. You shouldn't sacrifice the here and now for the future. If you don't manage your present well, none of those visions or dreams that you have of changing the world will ever see the light of day.

3. *Whoever causes others to become powerful is ruined because that power is due to either cleverness or force, both attributes that are not trusted by those who have been raised to positions of power.*

In Machiavelli's book, *The Prince,* King Louis XII made several mistakes that cost him Milan. One of those mistakes was not inhabiting the state after he had conquered it. When Louis XII made another grave mistake by bringing in a foreign power to rule Milan, instead of protecting his newly acquired state from the influence of foreign powers, many of her citizens were unhappy with him and allied themselves to the Pope. The hatred they felt towards their current ruler because they felt he didn't have their best interests at heart caused them to rally behind Pope Alexander VI.

Instead of securing his place, his absence allowed Pope Alexander VI to grow more powerful until King Louis XII became alienated from his subjects, and his power among them weakened, which made it easy for Pope Alexander to oust power from him. He did not live in Italy, so he could not quickly see these issues as they were starting until they became too severe for him to handle. In the end, he lost all his territories.

A modern-day example of a politician who allowed his absence to send his career and constituency to deterioration is Nigerian's president, Muhammadu Buhari. In May 2017, reports came in that he had left the country to the United Kingdom for unknown medical reasons and for 90 days, nobody in the country could say for sure where he was or what ailed him, nor could they ascertain when he would return or who was in charge of ruling the country. Before then, he had just returned to the country in March after nearly two months away in London.

His continued absence sparked outrage among members of the Nigerian community, both online and offline. Many Nigerians were worried about how effective the president was and who took critical time-sensitive decisions in his absence as the country was experiencing several economic uncertainty and difficulties caused by delays in making vital policy decisions.

As a result, the country split into two factions, with one group calling for the president to either return to his duty or resign and the other defending his right to seek medical care overseas if he so wished. People took it as far as storming the streets to demonstrate the president's absence. He eventually returned, but the damage had already been done. He had lost the trust and confidence of a large portion of his electorates.

Remaining present or letting your presence be felt is a great way to build confidence among the people you lead and to prevent confusion and division among them.

Chapter Eleven

Gaining Cooperation: Is It Better To Be Feared or Loved?

"It is safer to choose being feared over being loved." - Niccolò Machiavelli.

One thing about politics is that the people you lead play a role as important as yours as the leader. Without them, your position is practically useless. It is every politician's dream to have the support and cooperation of the people, whether they have the same ideologies or not. You can either win their cooperation through the love they have for you or force it through their fear of you.

On the topic of being loved or feared by the people you lead, Machiavelli gave some interesting points that should bear mentioning.

> 1. *Coming down to the other qualities mentioned above, I say that every prince should expect himself to be seen as benevolent and not ruthless. However, the prince must be careful not to allow his mindedness to be abused.*

Popularity is a major factor in the success of a politician or political party. Every politician wants to remain popular among the people. They want the people to see them as accessible, thoughtful, generous, considerate, caring, compassionate, and friendly.

They want every news story to capture their more human side, to show them caring for people, helping their community, serving in happiness, and reaching out to local charities.

Public relation is very important, and that's what Machiavelli highlighted in the quote, *"every prince should expect himself to be seen as benevolent and not ruthless."* The kind of reputation you have is very important. However, you have to be careful not to go overboard with it, or you will find that people will not hesitate to use your kindness against you.

> 2. *Is being loved better than being feared or feared better than being loved?" I will tell you immediately that a prince ought to strive for both, but because it is difficult to combine them both in one person if he had to choose one, it is safer to choose being feared over being loved.*

Machiavelli insists that concerning treating your constituents with kindness or cruelty, it is best for a politician to strive for the balance of both love and fear. However, it is almost impossible for humans to both fear and love the same person. If you had to choose between the two emotions, he believed that it was better for a politician to gain the fear of the people than their love, and we would get into his reasons for that in a moment.

Politicians always have to make the hard choices that their constituents would not want to make. It is part of the responsibilities of being a leader. Your policies cannot please everyone. So if you had to make the hard choice of choosing between sacrificing one for the greater good of the world or saving one person to the detriment of the world, you should understand which of these courses would bring less pain in the long run.

An example of this would be comparing the responses that Jacinda Ardern, the Prime Minister of New Zealand, and Jair Bolsonaro, the Brazilian President, had towards the COVID-19 pandemic. In the first half of 2020, when the disease was still under investigation, and not a lot of information was known about it, the WHO recommended lockdowns as part of the means to reduce the spread of the disease and buy more time until a cure could be found.

Understandably, this recommendation had a lot of pushback from people who were worried about the possible implications it will have on the economy, as most businesses would be affected by the ban, as well as its social and psychological impact. Some people felt that the risk of a few infections was not worth plundering the whole nation into compulsory isolation and others felt that if the result was fewer infections and deaths, lockdowns were worth exploring. While this argument was going on, valuable time was wasting, and world leaders needed to act fast to curtail the spread of the disease and reduce the alarming to the WHO recommendation was a hard decision to make, as either of the options would have angered some people. Some leaders, like Jacinda, were proactive in imposing the lockdown and banning flights into and out of the country. After sensitizing her people about it, she gained their cooperation and put the whole country on lockdown while working with scientists to create a more feasible solution. The result is that New Zealand has one of the lowest infection and death rates worldwide.

On the other hand, Jair Bolsonaro refused to place the country under lockdown because he didn't think the disease was deadly enough to place the country's economy in stagnation. The result is that Brazil has the second-highest infection and death rates in the world. The irony is that the economic suicide he was trying to avoid in the beginning still happened because the Brazillian economy shrunk by 5.8% in 2020, and World Bank predicts another recession for the country. At this point, even the people that supported him when he decided not to place the country on lockdown because of the negative economic implications would have changed their stance.

Two leaders in the same situation with two choices to be made, one chose to make the tough call that might cause temporary discomfort but less pain to the citizens in the long run while the other didn't, and the results were markedly different.

> 3. *The reason for this is that people are generally ungrateful, fickle, false, cowardly, and greedy. As long as*

you remain successful, they will remain with you, willingly offering their blood, properties, lives, and children when need is far away. However, as soon as the need arises, they will turn their backs against you.

Human nature is fickle. They will accept anything as long as it serves their selfish purpose. Machiavelli warns that people who appear to support you because of the favor they stand to gain from you will not hesitate to turn against you if the tides turn against you and the favors they used to enjoy stop coming.

4. *Therefore, the prince, as long as he keeps his people united and loyal, should not be bothered about the reputation of cruelty. With only a few examples, the prince will show himself to be more benevolent than those who, through too much mercy, allow riots that lead to killing and looting to arise. Such incidents are capable of hurting a large population, while the executions that could have quelled them would only affect a few individuals.*

According to Machiavelli, as long as whatever policy you are about to put in place ensures that your people will be satisfied, happy, and at peace, you don't have to bother yourself with earning the reputation of cruelty. Most leaders would show too much compassion and consideration to the point that it will cripple whatever tough call they have to make. In the bid to not estrange or disappoint the people they lead, they end up worsening things by causing more problems, disorder, and turmoil.

Once they taste benevolence, people will always want more from their leaders, but since they hate discipline, only one taste of it will maintain peace and restore order. Machiavelli points out that although cruelty may be necessary, you shouldn't overdo it. Just use a few people as scapegoats for well-used discipline or cruelty, and the rest will fall in line to avoid being punished.

Just like love, it is quite easy to overuse cruelty, and that defeats the entire purpose. Choosing scapegoats to take the brunt of your cruelty rather than punishing the entire population is an economical and efficient way to get your message across.

People who choose to be overly compassionate in the bid to remain loved are often not strong and assertive. Once you walk down that path, it can be hard to turn back. Once you have earned yourself a reputation of being kind, it boxes you in, and more people will expect you to behave that way. The moment you don't, people will see you as being mean, indifferent, and even tyrannical.

However, when people have a reputation for being cruel to do something compassionate, no matter how little, people appreciate it more. It is better to have a bad reputation and do the occasional good thing than to have a good reputation and do something occasionally bad. The former is seen as an improvement, while the latter is seen as a blemish.

Too much compassion can lead to overindulgence, while too much cruelty leads to hatred. It is best to use them both sparingly.

> 5. *Out of all princes, it is impossible for a newly crowned prince to avoid the reputation of cruelty. This is because new territories are full of dangers that need to be checked. Nonetheless, the prince must be slow to believe or act and should not show fear. He must act calmly with concern and empathy for his people, such that overconfidence does not cause him to be careless, and too much caution does not cause him to be suspicious and intolerable.*

Machiavelli adds that of everyone that will find it hard to avoid having a reputation of being cruel, a newly elected leader is top on the list. Usually, when people elect new leaders, they do so because they expect to see change. It is never easy to change things because, unlike what they will have you believe, people don't like change, and they will resist it. You will ruffle a few feathers in your line of work, especially newcomers that will have to fight hard to establish their position and reputation in their offices. Therefore, since you cannot avoid the reputation of being cruel, you might as well not bother trying.

However, Machiavelli did not promote unnecessary and extreme cruelty towards your people. In fact, he criticized leaders who were overly cruel and misused their power because it bothered on the line of mistreatment and abuse. As mentioned before, too much cruelty will not lead to obedience, cooperation, support, or loyalty - only hatred. If you are going to use cruelty, let it be justified, and the benefits have to be worth it.

6. *Any prince that completely believes their promises and neglects to place other precautions would be completely destroyed. This love is caused by the things they stand to gain and not by sincere or noble feelings. It may be earned but is often insecure and cannot be relied upon in times of need. People are less afraid to offend the one who is beloved than one who is feared. This love is held by a chain of obligation that, due to the fickle nature of man, would break at any opportunity for their advantage. The fear of severe punishment, on the other hand, never fails.*

Love is a powerful motivator, so is fear. While love creates a feeling of obligation or duty, fear instills obedience and discipline. The fear of punishment, imprisonment, social stigma, and retribution is what motivates people to obey laws. If people did not fear the consequences of flouting laws, people would act without discipline and control.

Every city and its inhabitants need a reasonable amount of fear for order to exist. Hoping that people will be well-behaved because they love you or because it is their civic duty is futile as none of these are firm enough to compel obedience.

7. *However, the prince should inspire fear in people in such a way that, even if he doesn't win affection, he cannot be hated.*

While there should be a price to pay for stepping out of line, it should be within reasonable limits. If you set them too high, it will encourage resistance, rebellion, and overt disobedience. If you set them too low, the price is not worth encouraging obedience and becomes useless. The price should be high enough to encourage obedience without crossing the line into abuse and mistreatment.

8. *His reign would endure without being hated, which will continue as long as he does not steal his subjects' properties or their women. When it becomes necessary to take someone's life, he must do it on proper justification and an obvious reason for it. Above all else, he must keep his hands off the possessions of others because, while people can quickly forget the death of their father, it is harder to forget losing possessions.*

Machiavelli listed some of the limits of cruelty; he said that in dishing out punishment, do not take your people's properties, jobs, offices, or honor for yourself. Don't attack their staff or their family members. It is understandable if you have to get your hands dirty while fulfilling your duties - that's what sets a leader apart. However, if you need to act, don't dally with it.

According to Machiavelli, people are more inclined to forget the death of a parent quicker than they would the loss of their properties. In modern times, we can call property reputation, honor, and any other thing people consider more valuable than family. If you tamper with any of these, the victim will never forget or forgive you, and these are the worst kind of enemies to have.

9. *Returning to the question of being feared or loved, I have come to a conclusion that, because people love according*

to their will and fear according to the will of the prince, a wise prince would do well to establish himself on that which is under his control and not in the control of others. However, as noted, he must endeavor not to attract hatred.

Machiavelli concludes by saying that while people may admire or love good leaders, they obey and respect strong ones who make all the hard decisions. People will love you according to their discretion but will fear you according to your behavior. You have no control over other people's emotions, but you can definitely control your behavior. It is best for a politician to base his administration on things that are within his control.

Chapter Twelve

Making Promises: Is it Better To Be Generous or Miserly?

"Nothing disappears as quickly as generosity because even while you are exercising it, you are quickly losing your power to do so." - Niccolò Machiavelli.

In line with the behaviors that a politician should be notorious for, there is a question of whether they should be generous or miserly. Should you donate to charity or not? Should you ask for credit or recognition when you do or not? Do you take the cameras along or leave them behind? Machiavelli answers these questions in his book.

> 1. *Of the two qualities above, being generous is better. However, generosity is done in such a way that brings you the reputation for it harms you. If a person is genuinely generous and is not known for it, such a person would not be able to avoid the criticism of being the opposite.*

He said that generosity was better than being miserly; however, being benevolent for the sake of it without it being known is a waste of money and does more harm than good to your political career. If you are a big anonymous donor and nobody gets wind of this generous streak, you will live your life with the reputation of being a miser when the reverse is the case.

If you must do a good deed, don't let it be anonymous, and there must be a purpose behind it. Be sure to get a photo op, at least, of your generosity. However, be careful with what methods you choose to show your benevolence.

Barack Obama is one of the most charismatic politicians in recent world history. Part of his charm was his generous streak. While he was the president of the United States, some of his most memorable generous acts to charity include the $50,000 donation he made to the charity organization CARE and his Nobel Prize, which provided ten different charities a total of $1.4 million to share.

Other charities that enjoyed Obama's generosity include the United Negro College Fund, the Appalachian Leadership and Education Foundation, the Hispanic Scholarship Fund, Africare, the American Indian College Fund, the Central Asian Institute, which promotes the education of girls in Afghanistan and Pakistan, and the Posse Foundation which helps non-traditional high schools get a college education.

If you look closely at all of these charities, they have a common theme - helping the disenfranchised communities in both the United States and the world at large. This theme served the purpose of further endearing him to all of these communities. It fulfilled three of the requirements that Machiavelli gave - let it have a purpose, let it be known, and be careful about choosing them.

> 2. *Therefore, anyone who wishes to maintain a reputation of generosity must be outlandish in his display of generosity. A prince who does this will use up his fortune on such acts and, in the end, would be compelled to unduly burden his people by taxing them and doing everything possible to make more money. This will soon make the people hate him, and when he becomes poor, he will be worthless to everyone.*

However, he pointed out that too much generosity will ruin you as human beings are insatiable and will always want more. You cannot meet all the needs that they will keep dropping at your feet. However, if you are the type that wants to maintain the reputation of being generous at all costs, you will have to give out more to maintain the degree of satisfaction that your good deeds used to bring.

The downside is that you will soon run out of personal and public funds living this way. To offset this decline, most politicians will tax the people harder to make more money to meet their needs. As with the previous chapter, people want to enjoy good things without having to pay for them. So you will discover soon that they will resent you for taking this route.

> 3. *It is either you are already a prince or on the way to becoming one. In the first instance, generosity is dangerous, while it is very necessary to be known as being generous in the second.*

During election campaigns, you can always expect politicians to give several promises to convince their electorates to vote for them. This is understandable because campaigns are a fight to earn a seat at the political table. Having a reputation for being generous is one way to get people interested in you. Politicians will make promises to cut taxes, build new facilities, provide better services, grant favors, etc.

> 4. *Also, if anyone should reply, "Many people have become princes and have done great things with the military and remained very generous," I would say, "Either the prince uses his own money or that of his subjects, or that of others."*

However, when they get into office, it becomes difficult for them to meet up with those promises, and that's because they quickly discover that while funds are finite, needs are not. Most politicians cannot afford to make good on the promises they make, especially if they also want to keep the promise of tax cuts, as the only available source of funds is your personal money or the taxes from your electorates.

> 5. *With his generosity having offended many but rewarding little, he will be affected by every trouble and run into risk at every sign of danger. Once he recognizes this and wanting to avoid this problem, he will be criticized for being miserly.*

When you run out of gifts or good deeds to give to the poor, they will turn against you. One, because you have outlasted your usefulness and have no worth to them anymore. Two, because your acts of benevolence will only benefit a few as they will, more often than not, target a small part of the community or special interest groups.

However, breaking the big promises you made, like increasing taxes to fund your little acts of benevolence, will offend many. People who don't benefit from them will be angry at you for using the taxpayers' money to fund things they consider frivolous. For example, if you build a new football pitch, the scientific society may see it as a waste of funds that could have gone into more research. If you construct a new park, the literary society may view it as an affront because they needed more libraries. If you repave a bad road, people on the surrounding streets may complain about not being considered. If you create a scholarship fund for marginalized demography, others may complain about being neglected.

You see, these are good deeds, but once you start doing them for one group of people, others will also expect you to do the same for their needs. But there's only so much money that can go into fulfilling all these needs. When you realize the hole you have dug for yourself and try to find safe footing by cutting expenses, people will call you miserly, and your hard-earned reputation ends up in shambles.

> 6. *If he is wise, then he should not be afraid of being labeled as miserly. With time, the prince will be appreciated more than if generous because it would become clear that the economy is in abundance, that he can defend himself from all attacks, and that he can carry out his*

projects without burdening his subjects. Therefore, it happens that the prince exercises generosity towards the many who are his subjects and miserliness to the few who he does not give.

Machiavelli believes that a smart politician should not be bothered about making generous promises. If that earns you the reputation of being miserly, so be it. However, if you can manage to keep the economy stable enough for everyone to benefit from it, and you can carry out your projects without placing the burden on your electorate, people will come to appreciate you better in time. That's because a large majority of your community will enjoy the rewards, as against selected minorities.

In 1988, when George H.W. Bush made his presidential nomination acceptance speech at the Republican convention, he made a promise to his electorate:

I am the one who will not raise taxes. My opponent, on the other hand, claims that he will raise them as a third or last resort. However, when a politician talks like that, just know that is the only resort he will have.

My opponent will not rule out raising taxes, but I will. Even if Congress pushed me to raise taxes, I won't. When they insist, I will say to them, "Read my lips, no new taxes."

As Machiavelli predicted, when Bush became president, he found it hard to keep his promise. On June 26, 1990, he admitted that he would need to implement several measures to improve the stalled U.S. economy, including increasing tax revenues. The newspaper headlines went wild the next morning. One very interesting one from the New York Post said, "Read My Lips, I Lied!"

It was not Bush's fault that he had to raise taxes. He and his team had been working hard to cut down out-of-control spending to generate more revenue, but, in the end, the only thing he could do was to renege on his promise and raise taxes. He had failed to do the one thing he promised the people he would do, and it hurt his chances at his re-election bid in 1992 when both his primary opponent, Pat Buchanan, and his election opponent, Bill Clinton, repeatedly reminded voters of the promise he failed to keep.

George Bush was not the only United States President to make campaign promises during the heat of the moment that he failed to keep. Throughout American history, you will find those failed promises littered.

1. Woodrow Wilson, in 1916, ran for re-election using the slogan, "He kept us out of war." Barely 30 days into his new administration, he asked a joint session of Congress to declare war against Germany, using Germany's broken promise to halt unrestricted U-boat warfare and an attempt to talk Mexico into forming an alliance against the United States as his reason. Two days later, Congress granted his request.

2. Herbert Hoover in 1928 promised everyone prosperity, including "a chicken in every pot" and "a car in every backyard." Less than eight months in office, the stock market tanked and plunged the country into an economic recession called the Great Depression.

3. Franklin D. Roosevelt in 1932 criticized his opponent, Hoover, for his deficit spending and promised to put the nation back to work. While Roosevelt's New Deal policies did place the nation back to work, it also increased the deficit spending more. In an unheard-of bid for a third term in 1940, he also promised the electorate, "Your boys are not going to be sent into any foreign wars." When Pearl Harbor was bombed in 1941, Roosevelt asked Congress to declare war on Japan, sending boys to fight another foreign war despite his promise.

4.	Lyndon B. Johnson became president in 1963 after John F. Kennedy was assassinated. While running for re-election in 1964, he painted his opponent as a war hound and promised not to "send American boys 9 or 10 thousand miles away from home to do what the Asians should be asking their boys to do for them." He failed to keep his promise when he sent combat troops to Vietnam and caused the war to escalate with his interference. He was forced to pull out of the 1968 presidential race after public opinion turned against him.

5.	Richard Nixon in 1968 promised to end the war and find a way to make "peace with honor" in Vietnam. His aides went as far as telling reporters that he had a secret plan to end the war. However, in his first six months in office, the United States combat casualties increased. He was not able to end the war, and it dragged on, even after Nixon was re-elected in 1972. The last American soldiers did not leave Vietnam until 1975 after Nixon left office.

6.	During his campaign in 1976, Jimmy Carter promised to solve the energy crisis, deregulate the oil and gas industry, increase the gas tax, and even pursue alternative sources of energy by installing solar panels on the White House. However, once he got into office, he couldn't find anyone to support or sponsor any of his initiatives, and the energy crisis worsened under his administration.

7.	In 1980, Ronald Reagan promised to pass a constitutional amendment that would allow voluntary prayer in public schools. Although he did propose the amendment, it died in Congress, and subsequent attempts to revive it in 1999 and 2006 achieved the same results.

8.	In 1992, one of Bill Clinton's campaign promises was to completely overhaul the health care system and provide universal health care for every American. During his first term, health care reform was a priority for his administration, but he faced pushback from the Republicans. He put Hillary Clinton in charge of the task force, but it failed to gain support, and the proposal died in Congress, despite Democrats having the larger percentage of members in both houses.

9.   In 2000, George W. Bush promised to privatize Social Security, reduce government spending, and "change the tone" in the White House. He also promised to prevent sending troops all over the world when he said, "if we don't stop sending our troops around the world on nation-building missions, we will have serious problems down the road, and I am going to prevent that."   However, under his administration, government spending shot up, partly due to the new wars American soldiers were fighting in Afghanistan and Iraq after the 9/11 attacks.

10.   In 2008, Barack Obama promised to work to "close the partisan divide in Washington." However, for several reasons, by the time he left office in 2017, the partisan divide in Washington was wider than when he entered office in 2009.

11.   In 2016, Donald Trump made several promises during his election campaign, including one to have Hillary Clinton imprisoned and to "build a wall" along the Mexican border with Mexico paying for it. He did none of these things in the four years that he was president.

All of these presidents had their administrations marred by the failure to meet up with the promises they made while campaigning. If they hadn't made them or had been successful in achieving them, it wouldn't have left a blemish on their time in office. If you are looking for a list of campaign promises not to make, this is a good place to start.

Chapter Thirteen

Invest In Good PR

"It is, therefore, necessary for the prince to have all the good qualities that I have described, but it is also necessary for him to pretend to have them." - Niccolò Machiavelli.

A s a politician, nothing can be more important to your career than your reputation. Machiavelli even says so himself:

1. *Nothing makes the prince more famous than his great achievements and exemplary gestures.*

While those great achievements and exemplary gestures could be about building and contributing to the community, they also contribute to building your honor, prestige, reputation, and glory.

That's the reason why during elections, candidates try to gain more credibility with voters by cozying up to well-liked, retired politicians. It is also the period where spin doctors weave the worst kind of smear campaign in the media to ruin the reputation of their opponents. If you are serious about your political career, it is important to invest in getting some good PR for yourself and your team.

2. *A prince should, above all else, strive in every action to be famous for being great and remarkable.*

When it comes to choosing who they feel is best to lead, people will consider both the character of the politician as well as their leadership capabilities. It pays to have an image that they can associate with the candidate - something that makes you more memorable.

Each time you step into the public eye, they will be on the lookout for the way you comport yourself, your speech, and the way you develop your narratives. Every eye, camera, and recorder will be on you, dissecting your every move until they find something to tear apart.

The presidential election between Hillary Clinton and Donald Trump is a good example of how letting spin doctors take your story beyond your control could damage your political chances. It is clear that Hillary Clinton suffered a lot of reputational damage due to several repetitional factors, including the email controversy. The opposing team pounced on that weakness and kept tugging until it left irreparable damage in Hillary's PR.

Although many people considered Hillary to be a very capable candidate, her reputation hung over her head like a shroud and hampered her ability to secure her position. They doubted her character, and that was her downfall. She worsened it by being evasive in her answers to questions about the emails, the data on her computers, her charity, and other areas. She was not able to strike confidence about her reputation in the hearts of the voters.

Public affection, human adoration, and voter support are very fickle. The reputation of a politician is one of the most fragile things on earth, and a simple mistake, an unguarded comment, a cheeky response to a question, or even silence when you should have said something could topple all of your hard work.

> 3. *I say that all human beings, when mentioned, especially princes due to their high status, are notable for their particular values that either bring them blame or praise. This is why people are known for being generous or miserly, generous or greedy, cruel or compassionate, unfaithful or loyal, soft and cowardly or daring and*

brave, friendly or proud, lascivious or chaste, sincere or cunning, easy or serious, religious or disbelieving, and so on.

This quote from Machiavelli matches the message in the previous chapter - human beings get a reputation, whether good or bad, for a particular personality trait.   This is especially obvious in popular figures like politicians.   The way they can get identified by regular people is through their singular, noteworthy feats rather than the general way they behave.

Even though deep down we know that human beings are multifaceted (that is, they can be both good and bad, generous and miserly, believing and doubtful), we would rather create a perception of them through generalizations.   If a politician makes the news for doing one or two noteworthy deeds, they get the reputation of being good.

> 4. *I know that some people will confess that it is praiseworthy for a prince to have all the above good qualities in him.*

It is good for a politician to stamp their name on something significant because that is the legacy that will be remembered in history.   People will always remember a politician that has any of the abovementioned good characters in a positive light.

> 5. *But our human nature does not allow us to have all of those perfect qualities.   Therefore, the prince needs to be careful enough to avoid the reproach of those vices that would make him lose his state.*

However, we cannot always display all of these positive qualities.   In fact, Machiavelli, with his usual pragmatism, notes that choosing to only display positive characters is an idealistic way of living when he said:

> 6. *Anyone who ignores the apparent reality for the imagination of what ought to be will sooner cause his*

own destruction rather than protection. A person who chooses to act completely moral will soon be destroyed among so many in the world who are not good.

The way that humans have to live in reality is quite different from the idealistic image that you may have in your head. There is no completely good person, so if you go around expecting people to be good to you because you are good to them, Machiavelli has this to say:

> 7. *A person who chooses to act completely moral will soon be destroyed among so many in the world who are not good.*

Politics is a cutthroat business. Everyone is on the lookout for ways to upstage you. Too much goodness on your part will bring nothing but destruction to you. The political world is filled with crafty people who will take advantage of your morality.

Just like choosing between being generous and miserly, you might have to choose between displaying more good characters that will bring you praise and bad ones that may bring you to censure.

> 8. *Hence, a prince who wants to survive must know how to do evil or not according to his need. So let's put aside the fantasies regarding the prince and discuss the realities.*

However, if you want to survive as a politician, you must learn how to switch between good and bad, according to your needs. That just might be the only thing that could save your career and give your community a chance to be better for it.

If it is necessary for you to be immoral, do it. If doing things that others consider wrong will bring about positive results in the long run, don't be afraid to do it. According to Machiavelli, there is no law that expects a politician to always act good - that is not a realistic expectation either. You must first weigh your circumstances and act in the best way that is profitable to your goals.

But then, if you are allowed to act badly, even though you know you will be judged harshly for it, how do you manage to maintain a good reputation, which Machiavelli also admits is important to politics, with the people? He answers that question with this next quote:

> 9. *It is, therefore, necessary for the prince to have all the good qualities that I have described, but it is also necessary for him to pretend to have them. I dare say this too, to have these qualities and to always exhibit them is dangerous. However, it is helpful for a prince to appear to have them - to appear to be benevolent, loyal, generous, religious, straightforward but flexible enough to take the display of the opposite of these qualities when needed.*

Since the way that other people perceive you is important to your political career, especially if your journey is just beginning, you can pay lip service to the idea of being good.

Machiavelli advises that even though you do not have any of the positive qualities that he describes, you should pretend to have them. Support a worthy cause if you have to; let your name be tied to positive things in the news, media, and on people's lips.

A modern example of a politician that invested in the best PR strategy is John Bel Edwards, the re-elected governor of Louisiana. In 2019, just before the Louisiana gubernatorial race, the incumbent governor launched a series of PR salvos that made him remain in the headlines and score free positive publicity with the media.

In Louisiana, all the candidates interested in the gubernatorial seat run for office simultaneously. So Edwards' opponents included a combination of eight Democrats, Republicans, and third-party candidates. The pre-election polls placed Edwards, former U.S. Representative Ralph Abraham from the Republican party, and industrial CEO Eddie Rispone, also Republican, to be the likely winners.

Edwards' campaign and PR strategy included using his position as incumbent to capture the media's attention while simultaneously denying or diluting the quality of coverage his opponents got. As incumbent governor of the state, Edwards held the highest seat of power, so each time he spoke, all of Louisiana's news media had to listen. None of the other opponents had the same advantage to command the media as he could.

Understanding this and seeking to use this to his best advantage, Edwards planned a series of actions that would make him remain in the news for doing commendable things.

He held a press conference at the New Orleans Saints training facility to announce plans to renovate the Mercedes Benz Superdome for $450 million. In a state that has a large football culture, this was a huge development. He also promised to help the only NFL franchise in Louisiana extend its lease for another 30 years.

Apart from being a strategic move that would improve the social and cultural value of the state, extending the lease for the New Orleans Saints franchise was expected to have an economic impact of $1.3 billion in 2019. Thus ensuring that the continuity of the franchise reflected positively on both his position as the governor of the state, in terms of job performance, and his position as an election candidate, in terms of community and state service. He would also stage several photo ops with Saints' head coach, Sean Payton, and former quarterback, Drew Brees. As a former high school quarterback himself, he would run through athletic drills, sometimes even competing with Drew to the love of the Louisiana media. The people of Louisiana loved football, and he had not only successfully positioned himself with two of the most influential football figures as a part of his campaign PR.

These PR moves served two purposes for the Edwards campaign. One, it served as a piece of organic information that dominated several news cycles and kept him visible to the voters. Two, it suppressed similar press events from his major competitors and other opponents, as they did not receive as much significant press coverage.

However, the biggest and most defining move that kept the media buzzing about him for days and swayed public opinion in his favor was writing a letter to President Trump to request a Major Disaster Declaration, which would trigger federal funds to help deal with the unprecedented flooding of the Mississippi River.

By writing that letter, Edwards not only created a newsworthy act of a state governor conducting state business and fulfilling the duties of his office but also proved his readiness and ability to work with the Trump Administration. Edwards was an incumbent Democrat governor in a deeply conservative state, which placed him at opposite ends of the ideological chain with the major stakeholders in the state. Although most of their ideologies differed, by writing that public letter to a Republican president rather than using other methods - like a private phone call - he garnered a lot of media attention.

By using textbook crisis management and news management tactics, Edwards was able to create and manage a relationship with Republican voters and ensure he had their votes. By showing that he was willing to work with bi-partisan forces to fulfill his responsibilities, he showed himself as one of the most qualified candidates to become governor.

Edwards example is one that shows that having your name linked to positive acts, whether in the news or by word of mouth, is a strategy that can be used for effective PR comms and news management. He also shows that effectively sustained news presence can successfully sway public opinions towards you and your cause as a politician.

It does not matter if you genuinely support these causes or you take them on as a guide to clean up your image or justify your actions. The only thing that matters is the public perception of yourself. You don't have to be good; just act like you are.

Citing Ferdinand of Aragon, the King of Spain, as an example, Machiavelli explained how one could cover bad deeds under a cloak of respectability and acceptance.

> 10. *In addition, he always used religion as a justification for larger schemes. He applied cruel policies to push people out of the Moors kingdom. We cannot find a more admirable or rare example than that. Using the same excuse, he invaded Africa, waged war in Italy, and eventually attacked France.*
>
> *Therefore, his achievements and plans have always been great and kept the mind of his subjects in admiration and occupied with the outcome. He continued from war to war, leaving his subjects not enough time to think about opposing him.*

Ferdinand grew his kingdom by conquering Islamic opponents and enlarging his empire; while acting in his own interest, he was able to cloak his behavior in respectability by pretending to others that he did it for the sake of his religion. So, people supported his pious cruelty as a necessary evil to bring more glory to the church.

Although Donald Trump may have spurred divided reactions to his promise to build a wall between the U.S. and Mexico in 2016, it gained him a lot of supporters. On the other hand, his democrat opponent, Hillary Clinton, in the same campaign made promises on immigration reform. However, rather than threatening to send immigrants back, she promised to offer law-abiding, hard-working immigrant families a path to citizenship. Her proposed immigration package would have liberalized future immigration.

When Donald Trump's detractors shut down his immigration ideas, arguing that building a wall and mass deportation of immigrants was unethical, racially inspired, and un-American, he decided to soften his stance and regroup so he wouldn't lose supporters.

He claimed that Mexico was sending their worst citizens to them and accused immigrants of being drug dealers, rapists, and drug dealers. In a televised speech, he claimed that every American was adversely affected by uncontrolled illegal immigration, and they were out of space to hold them to prevent them from joining the American population, so the wall would solve all their problems.

By spinning the media narrative to make it appear that he was putting Americans first and claiming that his policies would restore America to its previous glory, he was able to garner a lot of support for his anti-immigration stance.

He went on to chronicle a number of Americans that had been killed by illegal immigrants. He claimed that immigrant workers weighed down salaries and kept the American unemployment rates high, making it hard for Americans to earn a middle-class wage. He promised to create a hiatus where immigrant workers would not get jobs until employees had employed all available native-born Americans and legal immigrants first.

He cast Hillary as a candidate who cared more about protecting immigrant families than doing what was right to protect Americans first. He blamed his opponent, and Barack Obama, for the violence perpetrated by illegal immigrants against Americans because they supported visa overstays, sanctuary cities, amnesty, and the release of dangerous criminals. He also claimed that Hillary's promise to grant amnesty, Obamacare, Social Security, and Medicare to illegal immigrants would break the federal budget.

In his media interviews, he promised to put Americans first and protect them. He told the voters and everyone else who had special interests in the outcome of the elections that the debate of the U.S. immigration had only one purpose - to serve the well-being of the American people - and everything else was a very far second.

By the time he was done spinning the media narrative to paint his cause as good, he had already convinced the average white person (the largest population in the U.S.) that most of America's problems were due to illegal immigrants. He sealed the deal with a nicely wrapped bow by promising that America would not bear the expenses for building the wall because he would make Mexico pay for it. Even though opinions were still divided on his immigration stance, he had cloaked it in enough respectability to convince a large percentage of the population to support him. That, along with Hillary's shaky reputation, sealed the deal for him in the 2016 elections and ensured his victory.

Chapter Fourteen

Be Both Human and Beast

"If a prince is compelled to behave like a beast, he ought to choose the fox and the lion." - Niccolò Machiavelli.

Human relations require you to have complex personalities. There are times where you will need to be civil and times where you have to act on your baser instincts. According to Machiavelli, there is a time and place for both personalities.

1. *There are two ways to win - by the rule of law or by force. The first method is appropriate for humans, while the second is suitable for animals.*

Acting in a civil manner involves following the law and using it to settle your differences. It involves rational thinking and calm discussion - a method that sets human beings apart from animals. However, the law does not always favor us or work in our benefit. Machiavelli believes that in these instances there is another way to act - by force, which is the order of nature reserved for animals.

2. *However, because the first method is hardly ever effective, the second must also be used. It is, therefore, necessary for a prince to know how to use both the beast and the human ways.*

In situations where civility will not solve the issue to your benefit, Machiavelli proposes the need to behave in a more forceful manner to strongarm, frighten, and intimidate your people into doing things your way. It is good and reasonable to act compassionately, especially as a politician to the electorates, but sometimes being compassionate is not enough and you may need tougher measures to secure your position. These tough measures may require you to act differently and resort to an animalistic show of force.

> 3. *Therefore, it is essential for a prince to know how to use both natures, for one without the other is hardly ever enough. If a prince is compelled to behave like a beast, he ought to choose the fox and the lion.*

It is therefore important that you know how to switch between being a human and a beast, and more importantly when to do so.

If you need the instincts of an animal to guide you, Machiavelli suggests choosing the lion and the fox as exemplary animalistic natures to mimic.

A lion is known for its boldness, strength, and courage. However, it is not very cunning or sly and may not know how to slip out of tight spots. On the other hand, a fox is very cunning and can weasel itself out of any tight situation, but it is not strong enough for a direct challenge.

The fox is not just wily enough to slip out of traps but also smart enough to spot them early on, so it doesn't snare it. A fox will see through deception and smell a plot from a distance.

A lion is not only brave and strong enough to face challenges head-on; it is also large and intimidating enough to scare off other predators. You will need both of these personalities to survive the chaotic environment of politics.

> 4. *As the lion cannot protect itself from traps, and the fox cannot defend itself against wolves. Therefore it is necessary to become a fox to sniff out the traps and a lion to fight off the wolves. Those who simply rely on the lion do not understand what they are doing.*

Machiavelli suggests that to survive the wilderness of politics, you can't be one without being the other. You will need both the cunningness of a fox and the strength of a lion - both deception and force combined. Where deception fails, brute force will work and vice versa.

It is erroneous to rely on the brute strength of the lion alone because unlike the fox, it is not shrewd and discerning. What the fox lacks in boldness and strength, it makes up for with its wiliness, spotting traps and deceptions easily and evading them. This is particularly important in diplomatic issues so you don't commit any errors that could spark bigger consequences.

Strength alone will not bring all your desired results. There will be times where you will need more subtle methods of accomplishing things. It is like that angry kid that always pummels anyone that offends him in the schoolyard - no matter how justified he is in his actions; he will just be seen as a bully. Some subtle tact should be applied in taking down your enemies.

Tone down your strength with cleverness, cultivate both behaviors, and use either of them when the situation calls for it. A leader that learns how to harness the power of both of these traits will become a formidable opponent, as the polar weaknesses of each beast can be managed by their polar strengths.

There is a common theme in all of Machiavelli's advice - there is no acceptable or unacceptable ethics, just as long as it is the right situation to display such behavior. As a leader, you will have to behave in ways that your situations dictate. If your situation calls for you to be bold, be bold. If it requires you to be cautious and wary, then be prudent enough to apply wariness and caution. If you have to be cruel, then ensure your cruelty is warranted. Your ethics should always be flexible and willing to change with your situation.

Most people believe in having rigid principles that won't falter irrespective of the situation they find themselves in. But Machiavelli believes that obstinate rigidity in a situation that calls for flexibility will only hurt you. Do not box yourself into doing something that will have a negative outcome on your plans, even though you have made promises to that effect.

> 5. *Hence, a wise prince should not keep the faith when such a promise can be turned against him or when the reasons behind such a promise cease to exist. If humans were entirely good, then there would be no need for this rule, but since they are evil and will not keep their promises to you, you are also not bound to keep your promises to them.*

Basically, Machiavelli is saying that if it serves your purpose, it is okay to lie. As you can see from the previous examples of campaign promises, most of them are either outright lies or an embellishment of the truth. They serve one purpose only - the people want to hear them, so politicians make the promises whether or not they can meet up with them. The promises usually revolve around reducing taxes or reducing government spending because that's what people want to hear. That's what gets you voted in. Nowhere in history has a person won an election by promising to raise taxes.

However, Machiavelli is not saying that politicians should always make promises they cannot keep. What he means is that if after you make a promise and the premise for making the promise ceases to exist or that it could be your undoing, you shouldn't feel the slightest bit guilty about breaking your word.

If you make a promise, you fully intend to keep but later reneged on it with good justification, that's not lying. This is a valid technique for survival in politics.

Machiavelli insists that if your situation finds it prudent for you to break your word, you can get away with doing it. He justifies this by saying if people were truly always good and kept their promises, then there would be no need for this rule. However, the reality is that most people will not keep their promises because they will chase their selfish interests first, then while you have to look out for both your best interests and those of the people you lead.

> 6. However, a prince ought to know the cleverness to disguise this behavior and be a good actor. Humans are so simple and, therefore, only concerned with present necessities, such that anyone who seeks to deceive will always find one person who will allow himself to be deceived.

However, people will not take too kindly to discovering that they have been hoodwinked or deceived. That sort of clever manipulation might not be seen as a strength, so be careful of how you present your wiliness. In a world where it is hard to trust anyone, you cannot afford to give yourself the reputation of a sly. So, if you can, hide your true intentions.

Do everything you can to remain in power, protect the people you lead, and ensure that the plans you have for them come to fruition. Be both cunning and bold.

An example of a politician that was so glib, he practically arm-twisted his opponents to win votes was Lyndon B. Johnson. One of his most notable feats won by arm twisting was an important vote he won from Senator Everett Dirksen.

In 1963, Lyndon Johnson became the President of the United States after John F. Kennedy was assassinated and inherited the Civil Rights bill from his predecessor. Kennedy had been trying to get the bill signed into law but couldn't quite get past partisan and segregationist Southern politicians who dominated Congress.

However, because Johnson had once been a player for that team, he knew the best way to play against the Southerners and beat them at their game. When he was a junior senator from Texas, Johnson had been part of the southern anti-Civil Rights bloc. But fast forward years later, in 1964, there he was, running for re-election in a Nation that expected the Civil Rights bill. But Johnson knew how to beat the Southerners at their game because he'd played it himself. As a junior senator from Texas, he'd been part of the anti-Civil Rights bloc. But in 1964, he was trying to get elected president of a nation that expected the enactment of a Civil Rights bill.

The Civil Rights bill was the object of the longest filibuster in the United States Senate history, designed to procrastinate or block the Senate from approving it. It took a whole 57 days.

Back then, one would require 67 votes to break a filibuster. As mentioned, all the Southern States were represented by Democrats who were opposed to civil rights, so even though they belonged to the same party, Johnson had to hope from those quarters. All hope lay in getting the 33 Republican senators to vote. To do that, he knew he had to cozy up to Dirksen, who was the Senate Minority Leader and win him over. Dirksen had promised Johnson's predecessor to allow a floor vote on the bill, but when the bill got to the Senate, he stalled. Dirksen requested a few changes from Johnson that would have weakened fair employment sections and public accommodations in return, but he refused to make a compromise.

So Johnson approached Senator Hubert Humphrey of Minnesota, the bill's floor leader, and told him they all knew that the bill wouldn't pass until they got Dirksen on their side. So he told Humphrey that they were going to do everything they could to get him on their side.

As part of their crafty plan to get Dirksen on board, Humphrey went on Meet the Press and praised Dirksen's statesmanship. He said:

> *"He [Dirksen] is a man who thinks of his country before he thinks of his party. I sincerely believe that when Senator Dirksen finds himself in a situation where his decision, leadership, and*

influence would be required to get us the votes needed to pass this bill, he will not be found wanting."

There, they had managed to get Dirksen into a fine spot. If he couldn't get the Senate to sign the bill, Humphrey had created a target to collect all the blame. To seal the deal, Johnson reminded Dirksen that he not only led the Party of Lincoln but also represented Lincoln's home state. As the filibuster went on, several clergymen thronged into the Capitol, trying to lobby senators to vote for civil rights, until finally, after pressure from all ends, Dirksen gave in.

Johnson allowed him to make a few harmless amendments to the bill to make it look like he contributed to its creation. Dirksen would later tell reporters that he finally realized that it was time, and he could no longer be in the way of an idea whose time had come.

Dirksen agreed that it was time to call for cloture to end the filibuster. He called Senator Richard of Georgia and told him they had gone far enough; it was time to end it. Next, he placed a call to Johnson and promised to do all he could to get the bill signed and get the whole deal wrapped up.

The motion for the cloture was approved, and the votes were 71-29 in favor of signing the bill. Twenty-seven of those in favor were Republicans that threw their weight in because of Dirksen. The Civil Rights Act may just have completed the work begun by Abraham Lincoln, but it couldn't have passed the Senate if it didn't have the support of a Senator from Lincoln, and that couldn't have happened without the subtle maneuvering from Johnson. In a call with Dirksen, Johnson told him:

"You're worthy of the 'Land of Lincoln,' and the man from Illinois is going to pass the bill, and I'll see that you get proper attention and credit."

Chapter Fifteen

Build Political Alliances

"A prince is also respected when he is a true friend or an absolute enemy."
- Niccolò Machiavelli.

The people you choose to align yourself with are equally as important as your opponents. Any politician that takes a firm stand on who their friends and enemies are is respected. Even when they lose, people will recognize that they made an attempt. Machiavelli was against neutrality and indecisiveness when it came to choosing who to align with. He said:

> 1. *In either case, it would always be beneficial for the prince to assist one of them to actively wage war. If the prince does not declare himself, he will fall prey to the conqueror. Then, the loser will be pleased and happy. As for the prince, there is no reason to ask for help, nor anything to protect or shelter him.*

When it is time to choose an ally to throw you back behind, Machiavelli suggests that you take a stand. Worrying about losing face because you chose the wrong ally will only be to your own disadvantage because neither winner nor the loser will respect you for deferring or remaining neutral.

> 2. *For whoever wins will not want people he doubts would help in difficult times, and the loser will not be willing to*

protect him because the prince was not willing to bring his troops to share his fate.

That is because anyone who wins will not be willing to align themselves to a flaky person who may bail out on them in difficult times, and the loser will not be willing to be yoked with you because you will not hesitate to leave them to their fate.

Of course, if you are in a position of influence, people will lobby you for either your support or neutrality in key situations. To handle this situation, Machiavelli says:

> 3. *So it always happens that the people who are not your friend will ask for your neutrality, while your friends will beg you to hold your weapon by their side. The weak princes, in order to avoid the present danger, often go neutral and are often defeated. But when the prince bravely declares in favor of one side and if his side wins, even though the conqueror may be strong and have the prince at his mercy, he would still be indebted to the prince, and a friendship is established.*

You have nothing to lose by choosing to take a stand for someone or even supporting them. If the endeavor is successful, it will forever remain in your debts, and you can use it later to further other initiatives.

> 4. *Victories, after all, are never so clear that the winner must not show some regard, especially justice. But if one who the prince supports is defeated, the prince will be protected by them, and when it is possible, he may assist the prince, and they both become companions on a fortune that may come again.*

However, it is always better to be on the winning team rather than the losing one. This is because the winners get to choose the kind of treatment the losers get.

> 5. *When the two neighboring powers go to war, but the prince does not feel threatened by whoever wins, it is even of more importance for the prince to support one side. By so doing, the prince helps to sabotage one side by helping the other. With the prince's necessary help and interference, the winner will always be indebted to him.*

Machiavelli says that powerful alliances are created by appealing to the self-interest of a more influential and powerful politician. But when choosing who to side with, be careful with your choice. Whether they win or lose, people with more power can crush you, and an alliance with them may not always be in your best interest.

> 6. *However, it must be noted here that the prince should never ally himself with someone stronger than him to fight someone else unless absolutely necessary. As said before, if he wins, he becomes his prisoner. A prince must avoid, as much as he can, being in a position of indebtedness to anyone.*

Machiavelli further says that an alliance with people more powerful than you should only be brokered when it is absolutely necessary. Whether you win or lose, you will be the one indebted to them, and that is never a good position to bargain from.

Chapter Sixteen

Be Wary Of People Who Support You For Their Personal Gain

"The prince must always listen to advice, but only when he wants, not when others want it." - Niccolò Machiavelli.

O ne of the things you have to look out for is flatterers and silver-tongued sycophants who only flock around you for their personal gain. You know them - the ones who always have a ready compliment, who always have sweet words to butter you up and make you feel good. While you bask in their adoration, they are looking for ways to deceive and destroy you. Machiavelli has some choice words to say about them:

> 1. *I don't want to leave out an important matter because it is a difficult danger for the princes to watch out unless they are very careful and discerning. These are the flatterers that every court is filled.*

You see them in droves, hanging within the halls of government looking for an unsuspecting person to leech on to. They do not do this because they care about you or genuinely believe what they say, but to see how many personal benefits they can milk out of you by ingratiating themselves to you.

> 2. *Because people are so wrapped up in their own affairs or deceived within them, it is difficult to protect themselves*

from this danger. If they want to protect themselves, they risk being despised.

The sad truth is that more often than not, it works. People fall victim to the deception because they are so wrapped up in their own heads. They do not like being told they have made a mistake, so they would rather believe lies that call them infallible. The truth may hurt, but lies destroy.

3. *The only way to protect oneself from flattery is for people to understand that letting the prince know the truth is not offensive.*

If you do not make the people around you understand that it is okay for them to tell you the truth, even though you might not like it, you leave yourself vulnerable and open to flattery, lies, and deception.

4. *However, when everyone feels free to speak the truth, the prince's respect fades away. Therefore, a wise prince should hold a third method by choosing wise people in the country and giving only them the freedom to speak the truth. Even then, they can only speak the truth of the things the prince asks and not say anything else. But the prince should ask them about everything and listen to their presentation, and afterward, he can conclude himself.*

However, Machiavelli warns that allowing any and every one to speak to you in a blunt, free, and familiar manner breeds disrespect. When you limit the number of people that get to talk to you freely, it reduces the dangers of overfamiliarity. In addition, it reduces the opportunities they have to gang up against you to pursue their self-interests.

Choose a trusted person among the several paying you court and encourage them to be honest and open with you, but only at your request. And if you ask them to talk to you truthfully about something, listen to them but make your own conclusions after. If their recommendations do not tally with the plans you have, do not hesitate to discard them. But if you find wisdom in their speech, then take it.

> 5. *With these councilors, both individually and collectively, the prince must behave in such a way that each of them should know that the more freely they speak, the more they will be preferred. Outside of this group, the prince doesn't need to listen to anyone but pursue what has been settled and stick to his decision. Any prince who does otherwise will be buried in his career by flattery or often changes his mind because of different opinions and be laughed at.*

There is a popular saying that goes, "flattery gets you nowhere," but according to Machiavelli, that is not true because flattery does, indeed, get people somewhere. When it comes to climbing the social ladder, flattery gets people everywhere - including your good graces - and gains them favors. It is an important tool for personal advancement because people understand that you will need all the help and support you can get, especially as a newbie.

In 1869, President Ulysses Grant went from being a war hero to the president. From the moment he resumed office until his last day of office, his administration was under attack from users and supporters who were ready to take advantage of his naivety when it came to political issues.

The first of the beginning of his woes began when financiers who had wormed their way into his good graces tried to corner the gold market, which led to the 1869 gold panic. Then in 1872, it was discovered that some shareholders of the Union Pacific Railroad had been bribing lawmakers to win contracts for new rail lines. One of the lawmakers implicated in the scandal was Schuyler Colfax, Grant's vice president. Since that was a re-election year, he was later dropped from the presidential ticket.

Even with all these scandals, Grant won his re-election bid because he was revered as a beloved Civil War hero. So people overlooked the many corruption scandals that came with his administration. They blamed the corruption on Grant's disloyal friends whom he gave federal appointments.

However, he didn't learn his lessons in choosing better bedfellows and counsel.

He appointed another old friend, General John McDonald, as the supervisor for the Treasury Department's internal revenue operations. He got the job as a means to boost Republican efforts to re-elect the president. However, his presence there did more harm than good to Grant's political career.

McDonald created whiskey rings in different parts of the country to siphon funds from the federal tax of 70 cents per gallon on alcohol sales. This he did by underreporting alcohol sales, manipulating figures, and funneling the extra money to the Republican Party. After Grant's re-election in 1872, the whiskey rings became a full-blown criminal operation that had many government officials and whiskey distillers profiting. All of it without Grant's knowledge.

When a new Treasury Secretary, Benjamin Bristow, was chosen in mid-1874, he discovered that more than $4 million was missing in tax revenue in the two years that McDonald was head.

He discovered coded telegram messages and unraveled evidence that proved the corruption went as deep as Grant's personal secretary, General Orville Babcock.

When Bristow took all of his accumulated evidence to President Grant, he refused to believe that people so close to him, people he trusted, could be capable of such nefarious acts. He had fought side-by-side with Babcock in the Civil War and genuinely believed he knew everything about his closest friend. Determined that there was more to the story and someone was playing something foul with the entire situation, he encouraged Bristow to keep digging and gathering more evidence. In his words, "if it can be avoided, let no guilty man escape."

To prove that there was no conflict of interest, he appointed the first special prosecutor in the U.S., Senator John B. Henderson, a Republican from Illinois and another Civil War veteran. He assembled a grand jury in St. Louis and began to indict and convict a large number of people involved in the scam. Among those sent to jail was McDonald.

To show there wasn't any conflict of interest, Grant appointed America's first special prosecutor. He was Republican Sen. John B. Henderson of Illinois, another Civil War veteran. Henderson convened a grand jury in St. Louis and soon began indicting and convicting scores of people. McDonald was among those who went to jail.

However, the moment the prosecutor started focusing on Babcock as well as other members of his family, Grant raised objections. Other Republicans also joined in the objections claiming there was a conspiracy to get to the president through his loved ones and friends.

In mid-December of 1875, Henderson was finally able to indict Babcock on charges of fraud against the American government. In his remarks to the court, he also hinted at interference and obstruction from the president. In anger, Grant ordered the Attorney General to fire Henderson, which he did on the basis that Henderson cast doubt on the president without any reason.

That proved to be a big misstep on the president's part as firing Henderson set off a public outcry, especially in democratic circles. People took to the streets to protest. One newspaper taunted Grant with his own words, saying he meant, "Let no guilty man escape unless he lives in the palace." When interviewed, Henderson told the New York Herald that he believed Grant's madness and thirst for revenge on hearing he had indicted his friend caused him to fire him.

Things were not looking good for the president, but instead of taking a step back to handle issues more diplomatically, he dug his foot in and blamed everyone for the mess, everyone except the people apparently responsible for it. He accused the press of being biased and fueling controversy. He tried to muzzle the press by asking the Attorney General to bring them before a grand jury to substantiate their claims. Grant was on a mission - one of self-destruction. At one point, he even tried to stop the prosecutors from giving key witnesses immunity for their testimony.

Grant had reached a state of full-blown hysteria and paranoia, complaining to anyone that would listen that the prosecution was targeting him and putting him on trial. Meanwhile, he adamantly defended his friend, Babcock, insisting that he was innocent. At a cabinet meeting, he declared that he would go down to St. Louis to testify at Babcock's trial, stunning everyone present. It was later agreed by cabinet members from both parties that the president should be questioned at the White House instead. In February 1876, Ulysses Grant became the first and only president of the United States to ever testify at a criminal trial.

The president's involvement in the case caused it to draw sensational attention, even rivaling O.J. Simpson's trial. Reporters came into the St. Louis courtroom from all over the country, waiting to hear the final verdict on the issue.

Babcock was eventually acquitted by the jury due to the president's testimony, to a large extent. However, he was forced to resign from his position in the White House. Of all the major targets probed for their involvement in the fraud, Babcock was the only one that walked away scot-free. The prosecutors were able to recover more than $3 million dollars from the stolen money and send over a hundred men to jail.

For the role he played in the outcome of the verdict, many Democratic newspapers called for Grant to be indicted for obstructing justice, but he was never punished for it.

The world of politics is very rife with duplicitous people looking for any means to benefit from you. Like Grant's story, even people you think you can trust with your life will not hesitate to use you for their personal gain if the opportunity calls for it. The problem is that they will more often than not drag you to your doom.

Grant was a war hero, but an excellent judge of character he was not. He was not equipped to spot these flatterers and users for who they were, and that made him an easy victim for unscrupulous men to take advantage of.

> 6. *Also, knowing that anyone, on any matter, has not told the prince the truth, he should let his anger be felt.*

The biggest mistake that Grant made was not standing aside to allow his closest counsel to be punished for lying and deceiving him. Instead, he chose to stand behind him, which could be interpreted as a reward for his bad behavior.

When you have selected the few people allowed to counsel you, warn them to avoid flattery or dissemination because you will not tolerate it. Otherwise, you will find yourself changing your plans to repeatedly fit the different whims of all your advisors.

Even worse than appearing to be a confused leader, flattery will cause you to make the wrong choices. When you get used to thinking all your decisions are fair and wise, when they are not, it may cause you to become autocratic and overconfident. You stop asking questions because you think everything is business as usual while everyone else laughs behind you for being foolish but keeps reassuring you that your decisions are wise to your face.

Machiavelli gave an example of a ruler, Maximilian, who almost never got anything done because of the differing opinions of his courtiers. He said:

7. *The emperor is a secret man - he does not communicate his plans to anyone, nor does he accept anyone's opinion. However, in putting them to practice, the plan is revealed and known. They are debated by those around the emperor; when they protest, he is immediately dissuaded from doing them. Therefore, the things he does today would be undone the next day without anyone understanding what he wanted to do, and no one can rely on his decisions.*

One of the downsides of flattery is the indecisiveness that follows. Maximilian was a man that kept his plans close to his chest, only revealing them when it was time for execution. Had he been one who followed through on his decisions, this would not be too much of a problem. However, Maximilian found it hard to follow through with his decision and didn't seek the advice of his counsel before he made plans.

Each time he brought forward a plan to be executed, his courtiers would argue in favor or against it depending on how much they stood to benefit from it, and at the end of the day, nobody would agree on a decision. They made a muddle of everything such that any plans that he started, he had to dump without anyone ever understanding what he hoped to achieve with said plans.

8. *So the prince must always listen to advice, but only when he wants, not when others want it. He must make it clear that he does not want advice unless asked. However, he must constantly ask questions and then be a patient listener about what he asks.*

To avoid unnecessary back and forth that will stall your project, always listen to advice. However, you should only listen to advice that you requested from people you trust and discourage unsolicited advice. And when you do get the advice you asked for, listen patiently and ask questions.

9. *There may be some who think that a prince can be wise not because of his own abilities but because he has good advisers around him. Such a belief is clearly false, for an unwise prince would never take good advice unless, by chance, he completely entrusted full control over to a brilliant and intelligent courtier. Indeed, in this case, the prince may be well governed, but it wouldn't be long, as such an eminent person would depose him within a short time.*

When you create a select group of people you solicit advice from, do not make the mistake of thinking that every wise thing you do is a result of the council received. Wise counsel is as good as useless in the hands of a foolish person that cannot recognize the wisdom in it.

So while your advisors should be honest, capable, and competent, you also play an important role in how their advice turns out. If your advisors are truthful and competent, reward them for their efforts. However, be careful that you don't give away too much of your power to them or you may not regain it. When a power tussle comes, you will lose your leverage.

10. *If an inexperienced prince takes advice from many people, he always takes different advice, and he won't know how to handle it. Each advisor will think about his own interests and the prince will not know how to control or observe them. This is obvious since people always want to deceive the prince unless they are bound by a necessity to be honest.*

Like Grant, it is easy for newbies to the political world to fall into the trap of rewarding their friends, allies, and supporters with positions of authority when they resume office. Like Grant's situation, that will only spell disaster. Machiavelli warns that having too many advisors and not knowing who has your best interest at heart will make it hard for you to control them.

Too many people will fight to gain your trust and get in your good graces for their personal gain and, in so doing, will become flatterers and users rather than advisors and supporters.

> 11. *Hence, good counsel, from wherever it comes, is the result of the prince's wisdom. Not that the prince's wisdom comes from good advice.*

In conclusion, Machiavelli says that whether the quality of advisors you have and advice you receive is good or bad depends heavily on your skill and wisdom as a leader. The advice does not determine the quality of a leader's decision, but it is the leader's wisdom that makes a piece of advice good or bad.

Chapter Seventeen

Avoid Hatred

"A prince is scorned if he is considered to be fickle, weak, indecisive, wicked, or lowly." - Niccolò Machiavelli.

The first thing that you need to have at the back of your mind is that it is impossible to please everyone. Some people will just not be appeased, no matter what you do. However, if you cannot get everyone to like you, it is in your best interest that the reactions you get from them are not outright hatred. Machiavelli said:

> 1. *Now, because I have talked about the important characteristics that a prince must display, I would like to briefly discuss under the general topic the things that a prince should think about to avoid those things that would make him hated or despised. If he can play his part to the best of his ability, then he needs not fear any dangers of other criticisms.*

If you behave in all the manners that a leader is supposed to and try to the best of your abilities to ensure that you are successful in every decision to take, you don't need to bother yourself about criticisms. Your position will remain secure - unless you are caught doing something that allows you to be despised and hated.

> 2. *As I have said, what makes people the most resentful is the exploitation of the properties and women of his subjects. The prince must abstain from doing both of*

these things. When neither property nor honor is threatened, the majority of them will live happily. Then, the prince only has to contend with the ambitions of a few that he can easily control in many ways.

When he discussed the different ways that a leader must act to gain cooperation from the citizens, Machiavelli mentioned that as long as you did not tamper with their properties, come after their loved ones, their honor, most people will have no problems with you. He listed that as a tactile line that must not be crossed under any circumstance.

Take care not to be caught diverting your citizen's finances for your personal gain. One way to make people hate you is to give yourself better benefits, a raise, or more perks than the common man, especially if you are working hard to get them to enjoy less. For example, cutting down costs in the budget, holding off on salary increases and benefits, etc. You should not be caught living lavishly while your people live in relative squalor and are worried about possible tax increments, inflation, and a fixed income. It is a thumb up the nose to people who already consider politicians to be more privileged and are already wary and envious of the benefits they enjoy.

Between 2013 and 2014, Ukraine experienced a series of violent protests that led to the ousting of the then-president Viktor Yanukovych. When Viktor won the elections in 2010, he was the people's messiah because they had been disillusioned by the Orange government that preceded his administration. He rode that wave to quick popularity among his citizens and would have remained the people's president had he done everything he could to avoid being held to contempt and hatred.

His first mistake came within weeks of being elected. When he chose members of his cabinet, instead of choosing members from both opposition parties to make up the seats, he filled them up with only headliners from his party. This sent a clear signal to everyone involved that his government would not be one of national reconciliation, defeating the purpose of electing him and disappointing those who switched from the Orange camp to vote for him. Thus, taking power and jobs from those who would have benefited from it.

Had he ended his mistake there, it probably would have been overlooked in light of his successful administration. In April 2010, he made another blunder by signing the Kharviv pact with Russia to allow the extension of the Russian lease on naval facilities in Crimea beyond 2017 to 2042 with an additional five-year renewal option in exchange for a multiyear discounted contract to supply Ukraine with Russian natural gas. The deal was widely criticized as a bad one that did not favor Ukraine at all and allowed Russia to gain control of Crimea.

Then he compounded it by signing a dubious constitution that ceded all power to himself in October. Within the space of 7-8 months, Viktor had gone from a democratically elected official to a dictator. It raised the alarm within circles that were more democratically minded. Had he had the foresight, he would have seen the pitfalls involved in becoming solely responsible for ruling a country.

The final straw that broke the camel's back was when he went back on the deal to sign the Ukraine-European Union Association Agreement that would allow Ukraine to join the EU and enjoy free trade, choosing instead to maintain ties and economic relations with Russia.

Viktor had set himself up because he proposed the deal and kept reassuring his citizens that it was as good as signed on his own end. He raised their hopes up as they saw it as an opportunity for both economic reforms and civilizational choice. An apt title because they were finally leaving to join the rest of civilization to progress. So when he went back on his promise, it was a big letdown to the people of Ukraine.

The Ukrainians were disappointed because they felt that Viktor had stolen an opportunity from them and took to the streets to protest in what became known as the Euromaidan movement.

On 24 November 2013, the police and the protesters began to clash. After a few days of protests, university students joined in the demonstrations en masse. Even with the snow and sub-zero temperature, Ukrainians were not discouraged - they had to get Viktor out of office.

In the early morning of November 30, government forces ramped up the violence against the protesters, which led to a surge in the number of protesters from between 50,000-200,000 in the preceding weeks to 400,000-800,000 on the 1st of December. The protests turned violent in response to government repression and police brutality that killed many and left others injured.

This went on for over a month. Several Western Ukrainian governor buildings and regional councils had been occupied by Euromaidan protesters. In several other cities, the protestors also tried to take over their local government buildings but were forced back by pro-government groups and the police.

Viktor tried to salvage the situation by having a meeting with key opposition leaders for constitutional changes and to restore certain players to Parliament. He also agreed to an early election by December. But the people were too far gone in their anger and hatred. On 21 February, an impeachment bill was introduced to Parliament.

When Viktor heard that protesters had taken over the country's capital, he fled to Eastern Ukraine, wherein in his absence Parliament voted 328-0 in favor of his impeachment and fixed a new election for May.

The only thing Viktor was interested in was enriching his own pockets from taxpayers' money. He and his family fled to Russia in February, leaving behind a trail of documents that showed how deep his thievery ran. By the time an investigation was concluded, it was discovered that Viktor and his cronies had stolen over $40 billion dollars in state assets. Three years after the tragic incident, Viktor was found guilty of treason and sentenced to 13 years in prison in absentia.

If Viktor had avoided being hated, he could easily have kept everything - the support of the people and his position.

> 3. *A prince is scorned if he is considered to be fickle, weak, indecisive, wicked, or lowly. All of these attributes should be avoided by the prince. In his actions, the prince should strive to show greatness, courage, bravery, and sombreness. In his private dealings with his subjects, let him show that his orders are absolute. He must maintain his reputation in such a way that no one can hope to deceive or manipulate him.*

If your electorate sees you as being weak, fickle, indecisive, wicked, or lowly, you lose all credibility. As said before, appearances matter even if you don't have the same personality. Once contempt sets in, it acts like cancer, growing and spreading until it consumes everything in its path and is hard to control. It could begin with whispers from word of mouth, an angry post on social media, and it will spread like wildfire to people that are already susceptible.

You become despicable as a leader if you become an object for jokes in the media or among your opposition. This is a valid strategy to ruin the reputation of your opponent because nobody likes or respects a leader who is an object of public ridicule. However, as the recipient of this kind of behavior, it hurts your chances.

> 4. *For this reason, a prince only has two things to fear - an attack from within from his subjects and one from without from foreign forces. Against the latter, the prince is defended by being well-armed and having food allies, and if he has good arms, he will always have good allies. Things within will remain quiet if the things outside remain quiet, as long as it isn't disturbed by rebellion. Even if he is disturbed on the outside, if the prince has learned to prepare and act, as I said earlier, as long as he does not despair will be able to resist any attack.*

However, regarding his subjects, if there is an external disturbance, the prince also has to worry that his subjects are secretly plotting a rebellion. The prince can easily protect himself from this by avoiding hatred and contempt and by maintaining good relations with his subjects. This is important for him to achieve, as I have discussed above.

When it comes to threats to their positions, leaders only have two things to fear - internal rebellion from among their followers and an attack from their enemies. Of the two of them, rebellion from your followers is the biggest and deadliest threat, and Viktor's story is enough proof. They see your flaws, know your weak spots, and know the exact place to attack you to hurt you the most.

Even if he were to be attacked by external forces, as long as his people do not hate him, he would be able to quickly quell it with an effective team and enough resources. However, a rebellious electorate that has given up on you will be harder to control as you are there to serve their mandate. You cannot lead without their support.

Machiavelli does not mean that you need to be loved by everyone to remain secure in your position but try as much as you cannot trigger the ire or hatred of your citizens. Polite indifference and grudging respect are examples of emotions that you can trigger in your constituents that are not quite hatred or love. Even a leader that has to use cruelty can get away with being feared as long as he does not overdo it and cause the people to scorn him.

Chapter Eighteen

Complacency Is The Herald of Doom

"A prince should not have any other goal or thought nor choose anything else for his research, anything else but war and its rules and discipline." - *Niccolò Machiavelli.*

Politics is a never-ending war cloaked in barely concealed civility. It is not enough for you to learn strategies to parry against your opponent and win, but also to remain prepared for war from any angle. You may not have to carry weapons into the battlefield, but you will constantly fight mental battles - in your community, on the council seat, sometimes, even with yourself, your ideals, and your weaknesses. The point is that losing focus even for one moment will leave you open and unguarded for attacks.

On remaining on your toes and staying one step ahead of the political game, Machiavelli had the following to say:

> 1. *A prince should not have any other goal or thought, nor choose anything else for his research, anything else but war and its rules and discipline. This is the only art that belongs to the ruler, and it enables those who weren't born princes to not only defend their status but also helps ordinary citizens rise to the princedom.*

There is no time to be idle. Even when you are not engaging in battle, you should be researching and learning everything that you can to improve yourself. Research on better tactics for battle, learn the rules of engagement in the political clime. Knowledge is indeed power. If you already hold office, knowledge can help you secure your position and remain in power longer, and if you aim to run for office, knowledge can help you climb steadily through ranks.

Any politician that misses the chance to learn the rules and apply self-improvement according to them is at risk of losing their reputation, status, or even more.

> *2. It is common to see that when princes who think more of peace than of war lose their state. The reason why they lose their states is that they neglected this art. Along the same vein, the reason they expand their territory is from the mastery of this art.*

When you become complacent and relax because you think you have already gotten the position you always wanted, someone else more hungry and prepared will snatch your seat right from under you. How conversant are you with the constitution? Do you know your procedural bylaw? Have you studied people that could be threats to you? Do you know enough about these things to catch your opponent off guard or deflect/counterattack when they try to catch you off guard? Do you have a mission or vision statement? What strategic plans do you have to work towards them? Do you have a code of conduct for yourself and your team? How do you sift through relevant and irrelevant procedures? Do you have safety nets and insurance put in place? Have you crafted your ground rules to reflect the legislation? The gag is that this is just the tip of the iceberg. There are so many other things you need to arm yourself with.

So you see, there is no reason why you should be idle and complacent as a politician. Every action you take should be intentional to bring you closer to your end goal. Each time your photo appears in the paper or on TV, there should be a motive behind it. Every speech you utter should have an intended target. You cannot afford to talk or act carelessly.

3.   *Among the many evils which not having arms will bring you is that it causes you to be despised. This is one of the dangers that a prince must guard himself against.*

We have talked about the pitfalls of being despised, and one of ways to be despised is by being unarmed and unprepared. A politician should be ready to think on their feet and the only way to do it is arming yourself with enough ammunition beforehand.

4.   *There is a big difference between the armed and unarmed. It would be unreasonable to expect one who is armed to willingly yield to one who is unarmed or that the unarmed man feels secure in the midst of armed servants. This is because while one person holds disdain towards the other, the other would be suspicious of them. Therefore, making it hard for them to work together.*

The general rule of thumb is that the most prepared player who understands the rules of the game controls the field and the outcome of the game. It would be unreasonable to expect the person who holds all the cards to yield to the other. What tools do you have around you that you can use to disarm your opponent? How will you keep yourself one step ahead of your opponents at all times?

Knowledge is one of the weapons that sets apart a successful politician from an unsuccessful one. The more knowledge you gain about the rules that apply to the game you are playing, the more ammunition you gather to fight your opponent on the field.

If you come on the field without adequate preparation and knowledge of these rules, others will spot that chink in your armor and if they know what you don't, they could use it to take advantage of your ignorance by scoring points that belittle you.

In 2010, Christine O'Donnell, the Republican nominee for the U.S. Senate in Delaware, was in a debate with her Democratic opponent,

Chris Coons, before law professors and students at Widener University Law School. Christine criticized Chris' position that creationism should not be taught in public schools as it was a direct violation of the First Amendment by promoting religious doctrine.

Chris' argument was that creationism could be taught in parochial and private schools but insisted that religious doctrine had no place in public schools. She lashed out at Chris for not knowing anything about the constitution and challenged him to show her where in the constitution the church and state was separated. Chris, clearly the more prepared candidate of the two, responded that the First Amendment stopped Congress from making laws respecting the establishment of religion or prohibiting its free exercise.

The moderator, noticing where this was heading, tried to move on but Christine dug her heels in and circled back to the topic and asked Chris incredulously, "are you telling me that the separation of church and state is in the First Amendment?", a gaffe that first caused the audience to gasp in stunned shock before they broke into laughter. It was laughable that a candidate seeking to be a lawmaker did not even know the Constitution!

It began to raise questions on whether or not she was fit for the role she was contesting. The voters must have agreed that she was unfit because she lost the election to Chris by a margin of 57% to 40%. The 2010 elections was her third attempt in five years for the Delaware Senatorial seat.

From this exchange we can see that communication can be a weapon too. You need to know how and when to speak, the right things to say and not say. You also need to know how to align your argument to get your message across and switch the game, as well as when to deflect questions, shut up, and when to go off the record.

> 5. *Hence, a prince who does not understand the art of war, among other mentioned disadvantages, cannot be*

*respected by his soldiers, nor can he rely on them.
Therefore, a prince must never let the art of war leave his
mind and, even in peace, ought to practice more than
during the war. He can do this in two ways, by action or
research.*

If Christine, on noticing that her opponent had the upper hand or
realizing the wisdom in allowing the moderator to switch the topic, she
would have escaped from the debate relatively unscathed. On the other
hand, Chris Coons showed just how important preparation was. He
was able to make his opponent look like an absolute fool without even
trying hard.

Even worse than looking like a fool in the presence of your opponent is
losing respect in front of your staff. Once they realize how easy you are
to fool, they will take advantage of your ignorance to push things that
will further their own agendas past you.

Machiavelli recommends that you learn all the relevant policies, laws,
bylaws, and procedures, and know where to apply them so you know
how and when to fight.

> 6. *In addition, it is advisable to practice as if in battle so
> that the body can endure and learn the nature of the
> natural terrain. The prince must understand the terrain
> of the mountains, valleys, plains and understand the
> nature of the rivers and marshes. He must learn about all
> of these terrains for careful analysis and planning. This
> knowledge may be useful in two ways. First, the prince
> learns to know his country and is able to defend it better.
> Then, with the knowledge and observations of the terrain
> in his country, the prince can easily understand any
> aspect that needs to be studied more.*

So, how hard are you studying? The internet is rich in resources that
can help you prepare. You can also use it as a practice field before the

main event begins. Go through blogs and social media pages, what are your colleagues talking about? Do you know anything about the subject matter? Can you share your thoughts on the subject with enough information to back your argument? If someone challenges you, can you flip it around and put them on the hot seat?

Christine is not the only person that has gone for office without knowledge of the Constitution as there are many who have come to the table unprepared without knowledge of their own political agenda and strategies, let alone policies and bylaws.

Because they fail to do due diligence, they go off track, making motions contrary to already existing ones and stumble to answer relevant questions during debates.

This unpreparedness is a big red flag on how irresponsible, ineffective, and unsuitable a candidate is for a position.

Voters can already tell that if they win, they will take the council on a merry chase that leads nowhere and wastes time and resources.

> 7. *But to exercise his brain, the prince should read the history and study the actions of famous people, see how they behaved in war, find out the causes of their victory or defeat in order to avoid the latter and achieve the former. Above all, the prince ought to follow what these famous men, who found someone who had been famous and praised before them to imitate, have done in the past and keep their achievements and actions in mind.*

You can never be too informed about a subject. After you are done keeping up to date with current practices, Machiavelli suggests that you go back to history to read and study the actions of those that have walked this path before you and see how they behaved, how much influence their behaviors had on their victories or defeat so that you can recreate the former and avoid the latter.

Read up on your local history. Check out political events from the past. How did the news report these incidents? Pay particular attention to those as it will provide feelers for your course of action.

A politician with foresight will be able to forecast where their opponent is headed by observing their actions and the reports from news articles. That way, when they make their move, you are not left scrambling to catch up, but ready to parry them blow for blow.

A wise prince should observe some of such rules. He must never remain idle during peaceful times but increase his knowledge in such a way that he is always ready to respond in the face of adversity so that when his fortune changes and bad luck comes, he is always prepared to resist them.

Chapter Nineteen

How Not to Lose Your Office

"It will be a great contempt for those born as princes to lose their country for their lack of wisdom." - Niccolò Machiavelli.

If it is your first time in office, chances are that you will be closely monitored by the media and general public compared to an incumbent. With an incumbent, they already know what to expect - their flaws, their strengths, their quirks. But newcomers have to first prove themselves and so they become a mystery that must be observed.

> 1. *The actions of a new prince are observed more often than those of a hereditary prince.*

Apart from the natural aversion that people have towards new changes, the people need reassurance that you will do right by them. They want to know that they made the right choice in voting you in and once you have reassured them of that, you will have their full support and loyalty, even quicker than what the former incumbents enjoy.

> 2. *When the new prince is considered capable, he attracts more people, and they are more loyal than the ancient princes. This is because people are more attracted to the present than the past and when they find good in the present, they enjoy it and don't seek more. They will also strongly defend the prince if he does not harm them in other matters.*

Machiavelli insists that if you don't ruffle feathers, pass too many restrictive laws, raise taxes, or trample on their rights, most people will be content and that contentment with what you are doing in the present will make them not to seek comfort in the 'good old days.'

So one thing you can do to not lose your office is to make sure that as many people as possible are aware of how capable and good your administration has been. Shamelessly promote yourself as an exemplary character for good governance. Be in their faces. Let your name appear next to many good deeds on the news, social media, and even blogs.

> 3. *So it will be a great glory for the prince to have formed a new kingdom and made the country rich with good laws, good troops, good allies and good leadership. Likewise, it will be a great contempt for those born as princes to lose their country for their lack of wisdom.*

Incumbents have several advantages over new politicians, and it is disgraceful when these advantages are not enough to assure them of a win. It is a stain on their reputation that they will not be able to get rid of should they decide to run for another office. To the public, that is ample proof that they could not get people to support their campaign despite the headstart that they have.

> 4. *Hence, our princes should not blame fate for losing their power after years of possession but rather their own laziness. In peaceful times, they never thought that times could change (it's a common human weakness that in peace, no one thinks to prepare for a storm). When chaos came, they only thought of running away instead of protecting themselves. They hoped that the subjects, who were disgusted with the attitudes of the conquerors, would call them back. This, when other things fail, might be good, but it's a bad*

thing to ignore all the other factors to choose this
course.

Machiavelli says that any incumbent that loses their seat does so due to their own incompetence and not because they had a turn of luck. They grew complacent, lazy, preoccupied, and failed to change with the times. Not preparing yourself enough for the future challenges that will come with your position will quickly make you lose your seat to another more prepared for it.

Chapter Twenty

How to Wield the Power of the Incumbent

"Unless affected by extraordinary or excessive things, all he only has to do is maintain himself in this state." - Niccolò Machiavelli.

T he power of the incumbent is an effective tool that allows a politician who already holds an office to be reelected. Like the quote above implies, an incumbent does not have to do anything extraordinary to remain - no brave acts, zealous reforms, or principled stands - just simple inertia from the electorate.

As long as it does not negatively affect them, people are comfortable with not making any changes in a system that already somewhat benefits them. That is why people will continue to vote for incumbents years after, even though they have forgotten the reason they chose them in the first place or they have become ineffective in office.

> 1. *It is easier to preserve hereditary monarchy, especially when the people are already used to living with their prince's family, than new ones. This is because most people will prefer the stability of customs that they are accustomed to over the new policies of a new ruling family. All that the prince needs to do is preserve his predecessor's customs and carefully resolve conflicts as they arise.*

Machiavelli believes that it is easier to control an office you already hold. As long as you do not introduce too many changes and stick to the status quo, you should get along fine with the electorate. You don't need to create innovative ideas because they could either be a hit or miss. Just continue as you were.

He is saying that you shouldn't rock the boat by trying to be innovative as your ideas could either be a hit or miss, and that is risky.

> 3. *Unless affected by extraordinary or excessive things, all he only has to do is maintain himself in this state. This way, if he loses his throne, it is easier for the prince to get it back when his usurper encounters misfortune.*

Machiavelli says that the prudent way for incumbents to act is to only behave in ways that will maintain their position. That is, keeping the same reputation and not jolting the public too much. Barring any extraordinary event, an incumbent will not lose elections and can easily remain in power, even when they are only average or mediocre.

He also adds that even though an incumbent loses their seat, they have a very good chance of being reelected if their successor makes enough mistakes to lose the confidence of the electorates. A case of "a devil you know is better than an angel you don't know."

Part Four

Fighting With a Team

Chapter Twenty-One

Leadership

"The general is the pillar of the nation. If the pillar is solid, the nation is strong. If the pillar is loose, the nation is weak." - Sun Tzu.

As a leader, you are the backbone of your political team. If you are weak, then your decisions and orders would be as well. This is why it is important to pay more attention to your opponent than their team. No matter how competent the team appears to be, the leader still has to give a final stamp of approval before they do anything. So if your opponent is weak, expect that everything that comes from that camp would be as well. If they are known to play dirty, everything that comes out of their camp would be too.

1. *We were faced with three challenges by which a leader can bring misfortune on his army:*

   a. *First is that if it is unclear for the troops to advance, but we keep them advancing, or we are not sure if the troops can back up, but we just tell them to back up. That's called tying up the troops.*

   b. *The second challenge is that if the position of the internal affairs of the troops is also unclear, by interfering with the military management, the officers and soldiers would be confused.*

c. *Thirdly, if the military principle of adaptation to circumstances is unclear, but you interfere with the responsibility of commanders, the generals would have doubts in their minds.*

All of these allude to one thing - that the chain of command from leaders to followers is broken. Leadership without a proper chain of command will only bring misfortune to yourself and your followers.

When World War I began in August 1914, the British and French were caught in a bitter stalemate with the Germans on the Western Front, while the Germans were beating the Russians, allies of Britain and France, on the Eastern side. So the British formulated a new strategy to attack Gallipoli, a peninsula on the Dardanelles Strait which opened up to Constantinople, Turkey. Turkey was an ally of Germany, and if they could take Gallipoli, it would be easy to take Constantinople, and Turkey would have to withdraw from battle. With the bases, they would form in Turkey and the Balkans, they could also attack Germany from the Southeast and weaken its focus on the Western Front.

They had created a wonderful plan, but everything depended on the victory at Gallipoli. The plan was approved, and Sir Ian Hamilton was called in to lead the command. Winston Churchill and Hamilton believed the plan was foolproof and they had enough men to conquer the Turks easily. The only order Churchill left was to take Constantinople; he left Hamilton to work out the details.

Hamilton's plan was to land at three points - the southwestern tip of the Gallipoli peninsula, north, and the beaches. From the very moment that the troops landed, everything that could go wrong did. The maps they got were inaccurate and they had landed in the wrong places. The beach was too narrow for the troops to pass, and the Turks were surprisingly fighting back. After the first day of landing, a large percentage of the army could not join the fight because they couldn't pass the beach without being pinned by the Turks. Gallipoli, that should have been an easy win, was becoming a nightmare.

When it looked like the plan had failed, Churchill was able to convince the government to send more troops. Hamilton created a new plan where he would land soldiers in Suvla Bay - a vulnerable target with a large harbor and few defenses. Attacking from this end would force the Turks to split and break the stalemate. Hamilton placed the most senior Englishman available, Lt. Gen Sir Frederick Stopford, to command the Suvla operation, and under him, Major General Frederick Hammersley would lead a division. Neither of these men was Hamilton's first choice, but he had to make do.

Hamilton's style of leadership was to tell his officers what they hoped to achieve with a battle and leave them to figure out how to go about it. Stopford made some changes to the landing plan, and Hamilton acquiesced. However, this time he made one request. Once the Turks heard about the attack on Suvla, they would rush to fight. He wanted the troop to advance to a range of hills called Tekke Tepe before the Turks, so they could dominate them.

The plan was simple enough but in order not to offend Stopford by interfering with his duties, he kept it as vague as possible and worse, did not stipulate a timeframe. However, his orders were vague enough that Stopford completely misinterpreted them. Instead of ordering his men to get to the hills as soon as possible, he told them to get there if possible.

When the troops landed ashore, Stopford's change in the landing plans muddled things up. They didn't know what positions to take and their objectives, and Stopford had remained on a boat to control the battlefield, so they couldn't reach him on time for confirmation. They wasted the whole day relaying messages back and forth the boat to work out the tangled mess of the plans.

Hamilton began to suspect things were not going according to plans, so the next morning, he went to investigate. On getting there, he realized that nobody had been able to do one thing right out of the plan they created for attack. Before they could rally together to fix the mistake, the Turks had already taken the Tekke Tepe hills and they lost their advantage.

Hamilton's plan was foolproof and would have worked but he forgot one important detail - the chain of command. A leadership with a broken chain of command will leave everyone confused and in the confusion, your opponents might find opportunity to harass you, like Sun Tzu says below.

> 2. *If the troops were suspicious and bewildered, the vassal countries would have the opportunity to harass. This is called self-disordered troops and it is to lead others to victory.*

Hamilton's troops threw away the one chance they had at victory because they were confused and running around in circles, which gave their opponents enough time to regroup and attack. A leader's job is to ensure the team remains clear on their goals, mission, and vision, otherwise, everything descends into anarchy that the opponent can exploit.

No matter how advantageous your position is or how well-ordered your strategy is, if everyone on your team is not reading from the same page, you will lose that advantage - just as Hamilton did.

Chapter Twenty-Two

Choosing Your Team

"The first impression that one gets of a prince is by observing those around him." - Niccolò Machiavelli.

T he first impression that anyone would have about you is your team. Before the public meets you to get to know you, they must have already had an interaction with members of your team. While you are the body, members of your team are the tentacles through which you have wider reach. In terms of how your team should represent you, Machiavelli had the following to say:

> 1. The choice of personal staff is very important to the prince. Whether they are good or not depends on the prince's discrimination. The first impression that one gets of a prince is by observing those around him. If they are capable and loyal, the prince can be considered wise because he already knows how to recognize their abilities and keep them loyal. But when they were the opposite, people would unfavorably criticize the prince for the grave error that he made in choosing the wrong person.

Just as the kind of counsel that you receive is an extension of your wisdom as a leader, the kind of people you choose to be part of your team shape your reputation as a leader. They are a direct and physical manifestation of your values and your sense of judgment. Everything they do is a direct reflection of yourself, so you have to be very careful when picking them.

If your team is capable and loyal, it adds prestige to your reputation but if they are the opposite, it is a big stain on your honor, and you will attract criticisms for making an error in judgment.

When choosing your councilors and other staff that will work closely with you, take the utmost care to make sure you have made the right choice.

Make sure that the people representing you as delegates on several boards are equal to the task and able to pass on your exact message without deviating to further their own agenda. Even better, make sure that even when you are not present or monitoring them, they can effectively manage your decisions and wishes.

It, therefore, makes sense that your team should be made up of wise, capable, and smart people who can do their jobs without micromanagement from you. The lack of micromanagement will help them do their jobs better and encourage loyalty because you have given them a position of power, honor, and respect.

> 2. *The human mind has three types. The first one understands things by itself, the second has to listen to explanations to understand, and the third doesn't self-understand nor understand when it is explained. The first is the best, the second is good, and the third is useless.*

There are three types of people - those who are naturally smart, the ones that understand that others may be smarter and listen to them to learn, and those who are too stupid to realize they aren't smart or who cannot listen to understand when people smarter than they try to explain things.

As said, the first set of people are the best because they work instinctively without micromanagement. The second set of people are okay because they are willing to learn and, with time will be able to stand on their own. But the third set of people are absolutely useless to you. If you cannot attract the first set to join your team, then settle for the second. But by every means ignore the third set of people.

However, in typical Machiavelli manner, there are caveats:

> 3. *He had the judgment to know the good and the bad when it was said and done, and although he may not have the initiative himself, he could recognize the good and the bad in his employees. He praised the good and corrected the bad. Therefore, they could not hope to deceive him but were kept honest.*

The first caveat is to make sure that you can recognize both the good and bad people on your team so you can praise the good and condemn the bad. That way, you can tell that they are not sycophants, flatterers, or fools.

How can you then tell the difference between a genuine employee or a sycophant? Machiavelli lists it as his second caveat:

> 4. *When a prince sees an employee thinking more about his own interests than prince interests and searching for his own profits in everything, such a person never makes a good servant. The prince could never trust him either, because he who has the responsibility of another in his hands should never think of himself but always of the prince and never pay attention to matters that the prince does not care about.*

Be on the lookout for employees who are more self-serving than being concerned about your interests as a politician. You cannot trust them to have your best interests at heart because anyone that has been entrusted to manage your affairs should not be bothered about chasing causes that do not align with your goals.

Early morning of June 17, 1972, brought about one of the biggest scandals that shook the American political scene when several burglars were arrested as they tried to break into the Democratic National Committee office located in the Watergate complex in Washington, DC. However, these burglars were not your regular run-of-the-mill robbers as they were a part of Richard Nixon's re-election team and had been caught red-handed as they stole documents and wiretapped phones.

Before the Watergate break-in, the political scene in America was deeply divided, what with the United States' involvement in the Vietnam War. So, for President Richard M. Nixon to get better chances at re-election, they needed a more aggressive campaign strategy. The members of Nixon's campaign team called the Committee to Re-Elect the President (derisively called CREEP), decided that illegal espionage would be the tool they needed. So they broke into the Democratic National Committee's headquarters in Watergate to bug the office phones and steal copies of top-secret documents.

The installed phone taps did not work properly, so on that fateful morning, a group of five burglars went back to the building to fix the wiretap. As they were preparing to break into the offices, a security guard on duty noticed that someone had taped over many of the door locks on the building. He immediately raised the alarm and called the police, who arrived just in time to catch the burglars red-handed with the new wiretaps.

When the culprits were first arrested, nobody made the connection between them and Nixon's team, but when during the preliminary search, detectives found copies of the phone number for Nixon's reelection committee among their belongings, it began to raise suspicions. So an investigation was launched to get to the bottom of it.

Seeing how the blowback from the incident could hurt his career, Nixon gave a speech in August where he swore that none of his staff was involved in the break-in. Because Nixon was well-loved and famous, many of the electorates believed him, and he won his reelection in a landslide victory.

However, investigations proved that Nixon was not entirely truthful about his involvement in the affair. For example, a few days after the break-in, he had arranged to pay the burglars hundreds of thousands of dollars in hush money.

Discovering that he was caught, Nixon tried to bury the evidence that has been discovered. So he and his aides concocted a plan to make the CIA frustrate the FBI's progress on the case. To cover up a crime of espionage, Nixon committed an even bigger crime - abusing his power as the president to deliberately obstruct justice.

Seven co-conspirators in the espionage were rounded up and indicted on charges relating to the Watergate scandal. Nixon aides urged five of them to plead guilty and avoid trial, while the remaining two were sentenced to jail in January 1973.

The case had begun to attract the attention of several people (including Bob Woodward and Carl Bernstein, two reporters for the Washington Post, John J. Sirica, a trial judge, and a handful of members of the Senate investigating committee), who had begun to suspect that something bigger was in play.

Around the same time that some of the conspirators had begun to sweat under the heat of the cover-up, Woodward and Bernstein got an anonymous tip containing key information from a whistleblower called "Deep Throat."

They had finally broken through and gotten to a few of Nixon's aides, including the White House counsel John Dean, who testified about their involvement in the affair and the role the president had to play in it. They even testified that Nixon secretly taped all the meetings in the

Oval Office, and if the prosecutors could lay hands on those tapes, they would have enough proof of the president's guilt.

Nixon tried to protect the tapes with his lawyers, arguing that his executive privilege allowed him to keep the contents of the tapes private. However, the Senate committee, Judge Sirica, and an independent prosecutor by the name of Archibald Cox were all determined to lay their hands on it.

On October 20, 1973, when Cox would not stop demanding the release of the tape, Nixon had him fired, which led several officials of the Justice Department to voluntarily resign in protest. This series of events became known as the Saturday Night Massacre. Eventually, Nixon gave in and surrendered some of the tapes.

By the beginning of 1974, all of the efforts to obstruct the investigation and the cover-up began to unravel. On March 1, a grand jury (appointed by a new special prosecutor) indicted seven of Nixon's former aides on several charges relating to the scandal. Not knowing if they could indict a sitting president, the jury named Nixon an "unindicted co-conspirator."

The Supreme Court ordered Nixon to submit all the tapes, and while he was still dragging his feet, the House Judiciary Committee voted in the agreement of his impeachment for abuse of power, criminal cover-up, obstruction of justice, and several other constitutional violations.

When Nixon finally released the tapes on August 5, it provided irrefutable proof of his involvement in the Watergate scandal. With impeachment looming on the horizon, Nixon decided to resign in disgrace on August 8.

When the Vice President was sworn in as president six weeks later, he pardoned Nixon for all the crimes he committed while in office. However, his aides were not so lucky as they were convicted for serious crimes and sent to federal prison.

John Mitchell, Nixon's Attorney General of the United States, served 19 months in jail for the part he played. The same applied to his Chief of Staff, H.R. Haldeman. John Ehrlichman spent 18 months in jail for attempting to cover up the break-in and the mastermind of the plot - G. Gordon Liddy, a former FBI agent -spent four and a half years in jail.

Although Nixon never openly admitted to any criminal actions, he acknowledged using poor judgment. It is obvious that his problems began when he chose the wrong group of people to work on his campaign team.

Chapter Twenty-Three

Organizing Your Team

"There has never been a new prince who has disarmed his subjects. On the contrary, whenever he has found them unarmed, he has always armed them. For when they are armed, those arms become yours." - Niccolò Machiavelli.

One of the first things you should do when you get into the office is to gather your team. Find competent people who supported you in your campaign and reward them by giving them a place on your team. Because they will only enjoy their rewards when you remain in office, they will become your staunchest defender in the community. Machiavelli explains it better here:

1. *For when they are armed, those arms become yours; those who used to be mistrustful become loyal, and those who were loyal remain the same; from your subjects, they become your loyalists. Although not everyone can be armed, when those who you do arm benefit, the others can be dealt with more freely.*

Arms, in this case, are not military weapons but the power, privilege, authority, position, and status you reward your staff with. Giving a few people the power to represent you in places is a way to arm them.

The ones that you arm will appreciate it and be indebted to you. Even those who do not benefit from gaining positions will understand the importance of your choice. He further says:

2. *Although the treatments are different, they fully understand. Those who are armed become your supporters, and those who aren't armed, accepting that those who have more dangerous responsibilities should have the highest reward would excuse you.*

Although the treatments are different, they understand and hope that in their continued support, you will also reward them with positions.

3. *On the contrary, when disarmed, the prince insults them by showing that he does not trust them, either out of cowardice or for want of loyalty. Both of these prejudices create hatred against the prince, and because he cannot be unarmed, he has to turn to the worthless mercenaries, as I have discussed.*

However, you have to note that once you give them positions, you cannot take them back, or it will cause them to lose face, and that will make an enemy out of your previous supporters - the worst kind to have.

4. *But when a prince occupies a new kingdom and adds it to his old one, it is necessary for him to disarm the newly conquered people, except those who helped the prince occupy the territory. These people, also, with time and opportunity, should be rendered weak and cowardly. Matters need to be managed in such a way that those who are armed in the state are only the prince's soldiers, who were raised in the old kingdom.*

So, where possible, put your own people in positions, especially sensitive ones, where they can watch your back and defend you if the need arises.

Be on the lookout for committees, boards, even staff positions where you think having an inside person will serve you. However, this does not mean that you have to completely fill up the position with your supporters and neglect the others. But you can slowly sideline and weaken their influence over time so that only your strongest supporters have all the authority.

Chapter Twenty-Four

Reward and Punishment

"To keep his servants honest, a prince must reward, honor, enrich, be kind, share his glory, and care for them." - Niccolò Machiavelli.

For this chapter, we will revisit Ulysses Grant's story in chapter sixteen. Machiavelli insists that the right way to keep your staff honest is to reward, honor, enrich them, be kind, care for them, and share your glory with them.

Ulysse Grant did all of that with his friends from the Civil War when he gave them cushiony jobs in the government as a reward for their association with him, cared for, and enriched them. Yet, it was not enough to make them remain honest and blame-free.

Does that mean that Machiavelli's advice had no merit? No, because he had an additional clause that said:

1. *At the same time, he must show them that they cannot stand alone.*

According to Machiavelli, in enriching and catering for your staff, do not make the mistake of allowing them to think that they have enough power to operate on their own. This is obviously where Grant began to get it wrong.

He gave his staff too much leeway and space, and with the wings, he had allowed them to sprout, they flew straight into the sun, dragging him along with them.

It is good to delegate duties, as it proves to your staff that you trust and respect them. However, remember that giving your staff rank means you have bestowed on them the power associated with it. The moment you give them enough power to get their head drunk, they could turn and use that power against you.

> 2. *At the same time, he must show them that they cannot stand alone. So that receiving a lot of honors will not make them want more, much wealth does not make them desire more, and many burdens make them afraid of changes.*

Power is a heady thing. Once someone tastes it, especially one that never imagined they could ever get access to that kind of power, it becomes a drug they cannot do without. They will keep wanting more. So to avoid that kind of conspiracy, Machiavelli advised that you show your staff that without you, they would be nothing. Make them understand that their continued reward comes from the longevity of your position in power.

Everything that Babcock got he did because of his proximity to the president, but he didn't understand that. If he did, he would have realized how his actions were direct jeopardy to Grant's position and therefore, indirectly his.

> 3. *Once the relationship between the prince and the servants is kept at that level, they can trust each other. Otherwise, the end is always destructive, either for one or the other.*

Machiavelli insists that once you have found that spot where you have made your staff indebted to you, then you can trust them with your heart and vice versa. Otherwise, they will take you down when they spiral into self-destruction.

Chapter Twenty-Five

Managing Your Resources

"It is better for one to lose with his own army than to win the battle with auxiliary soldiers, as you cannot consider any victory won with them as being real." - Niccolò Machiavelli.

W hen Machiavelli discussed this subject in his book, he talked about soldiers in terms of war, but in the context of politics, your soldiers are the resources that will help you to fight and win against your opponents - finances, manpower, media, campaign, goodwill, etc. When it looks like your resources alone cannot help you win the battle over your opponents, the temptation to call in reinforcements from other people you consider allies is always there. However, Machiavelli expressly states that in that way lies the danger.

> 1. *The armies that a prince uses to protect his nation are either his own or mercenaries or auxiliary or mixed.*

There are four ways with which you can use the resources available to acquire a political position. You can either use yours alone, loan from several people who have no skin in the game (mercenaries), use your biggest political ally as a support system (auxiliary), or maintain a system that mixes all of them together. However, apart from using your own resources and abilities, the rest have limitations that Machiavelli has so kindly pointed out.

2. *The mercenaries and auxiliary forces are useless and dangerous. If a prince holds a nation that relies on these armies, then it is unstable and insecure because they are disunited, ambitious, indisciplined, unfaithful, courageous in the presence of friends, and cowardly in the presence of enemies. They are not afraid of God and are dishonest to people.*

As he has stated, it is a dangerous thing to leave yourself at the mercy of others when it comes to resources because you cannot rely on them to always come through for you. At best, that makes your position unstable and precarious. At worst, that leaves you open for your opponent to tear apart completely.

If you have to bring in help from outside, it might be difficult to hold them united to your purpose and against your opponents. That is because people tend to be selfish and self-serving. They will always put their interests first, and if it so happens that your goals do not align with theirs, they have no qualms about throwing you under the bus completely.

3. *Destruction is postponed only as long as an attack is postponed, for in peace, they will plunder you, and in war, your enemy will. In fact, they have no other interest or reason for fighting other than a small stipend, which is not enough money to make them die for your cause. They are willing enough to be your soldiers while you are at peace, but if war comes, they either disappear or run from the enemy.*

Mercenaries are only in the game as long as they profit from it. Their loyalty goes to the highest bidder, so their support is very tenuous, volatile, and subject to change when someone with a better offer comes along.

They do not have any skin in your political war, so they have nothing to lose if you lose or gain if you win, so long as you give them their compensation for helping you.

They are one of the weakest links you could have - at war, your opponents can exploit them to crumble your plans, and if you are at peace, they could be the ones exploiting you to their self-interest. When all seems to be going well, they will remain in your corner to back you up, but as soon as the first sign of trouble comes, they have no problems jumping ship and leaving you to drown in the brewing mess. They are not reliable at all.

> 4. *I want to further demonstrate the dangers of these soldiers. The mercenary captains are either capable men or not. If they are, one cannot trust them because they always aspire to their personal greatness, either by oppressing you, who is their master, or others against your will. But if the captain is incompetent, then you are destroyed in the usual way.*

There are two ways by which the one who controls the resources you want to borrow can ruin you - by their competence and incompetence. If they are competent, they may begin to recognize opportunities that you are missing, or their greed can get in the way, and they will look for how to disenfranchise you to take your place. However, if they are incompetent, your ruin will come from the usual avenues.

Francesco Sforza served as a mercenary for Filippo Maria Visconti, Duke of Milan, and fought for and against him over a period of 20 years. But in that time, he started eyeing the seat of Milan, so he got betrothed to Filippo's only daughter and child, hoping to one day inherit the kingdom. However, his relationship with his would-be father-in-law was strenuous.

In 1434, Cosimo de Medici offered a large reward, including a seat in Florence to fight against Milan. Fighting for the Florentine-Venetian league against Milan, he won Verona in 1438 and defeated Milan in Anghiari in 1440. The next year, he married his fiancée during a period of uneasy truce. However, the truce did not last long, and he was soon fighting against his father-in-law again in 1443.

In 1447, the duke of Milan fell seriously ill while under threat of attack from a Venetian army, so he sent for his mercenary son-in-law to help. Before Francesco got to Milan, the duke died, and he found out that instead of willing the Duchy to him, his father-in-law had given it to Alfonso of Aragon, the King of Naples.

The Milanese took advantage of the confusion to rebel and proclaimed themselves a republic with Francesco as their captain-general. This sparked a three-pronged struggle between Venice, Francesco, and the Milanese republic. In 1449, Milan went behind Francesco to create a peace pact with Venice, and in response, he besieged the city and starved it into surrender. Therefore, in 1450, Francesco Sforza became the Duke of Milan after acting as a mercenary for years for the old one.

> 5. *I should have little difficulty proving this, for the destruction of Italy was caused but nothing else but relying on mercenaries for help for many years. Although they used to make some feats in the past and appeared brave among themselves, yet when enemy nations came, they showed us the truth about them.*

When the king of Naples, Ferdinard I offended Pope Innocent VIII by not paying his feudal dues to the papacy, he was excommunicated and banned from ruling Naples, and the Pope gave the Kingdom of Naples to Charles VIII, the grandson of the French King, Charles VII. This ushered in the French to Italy.

Just before the pope died, he made peace with Ferdinard and revoked the ban. However, the offer made to Charles VIII was still a bone of contention in Italy. There was also a third claim to the throne of Naples by Rene II, the Duke of Lorraine. The people of Naples had already offered the crown to Rene, but Charles VIII blocked it, saying he had more rights to the throne because his mother was closer than Rene's in the line of succession. In 1494, Ferdinand died and was succeeded by his son, Alfonso II.

That same year, Ludovico Sforza, who had been managing the Duchy of Milan, decided to claim it as his after showing a weak connection to the seat. However, Alfonso II challenged him over it because he also had claims to the throne. In the bid to get Alfonso out of his way, Ludovico encouraged Charles VIII to take Innocent's offer and claim the throne of Naples as his.

Charles VIII gathered an army of 25,000 soldiers, 8,000 of them being Swiss mercenaries, and blew through Italy to claim his seat. Thus, the first Italian war began, and it ushered in a slew of subsequent wars from other European countries seeking to take control of the divided Italian states.

However, Ludovico seeing how quickly Charles breezed through Italy and realizing his error in judging the French's power, became alarmed. Charles also had a claim to Milan, and he was afraid he wouldn't be satisfied with conquering only Naples. So he formed the League of Venice along with the emperor Maximilian I, the pope, and King Ferdinand II of Aragon to chase Charles out of Italy, and it worked.

However, the war already left behind its damage. The Italian states were weakened and left them vulnerable to the conflicting ambitions of both France and Spain. Charles' successor, Louis XII, seeing as he had some claim to both Milan and Naples, started plotting to invade the cities. The Venetians, having a short memory and not learning from their past mistakes, invited Louis XII to help them capture Lombardy on the premise that he would give them half of the Kingdom. King Louis invaded Lombardy, seized Milan, and quickly set his eyes on Naples.

Concerning the use of auxiliary armies, Machiavelli had the following to say:

> 6. *These soldiers can be helpful and good to their master, but it is a disadvantage to the one who asks for it. Because if they lose, the prince is ruined, and if they win, the prince becomes under their control.*

In the hands of your political allies, these resources may yield stellar results but accepting help and resources from them puts you at a great disadvantage. If they lose, you lose as well, but if they win, it places you under the control of your ally. They may want to use their help to cash in favors, some of which may be too costly for you to pay.

> 7. *Therefore, let those who have no ambitions to conquer use auxiliary troops, for they are much more dangerous than mercenaries. For them, your ruin is predetermined because they are all united and obey their commanders. But with the mercenaries, when they have won the battle, need more time and better opportunities to hurt you. They are unified, having been found and paid by you. Their commander is a third party installed by you, therefore, making it impossible for him to immediately have the authority to hurt you.*

Where the auxiliary soldiers become more dangerous to use than mercenaries is that they already have a functioning system and answer to one person that is not you. When you use the system of resources that your ally already set up, it is up to them to determine who they can spare to join your team, control the funds you receive, etc. - everyone is in their pocket. They can decide to sabotage you and will be successful because you do not have the resources to fight them back.

However, when you use several sources, it will take quite a lot of time for them to rally around a common cause for sabotaging you before they can act, buying you enough time to pull the plug on the plans.

Either way, it is clear that using any of these methods is quite dangerous.

> 8. *A wise prince will, therefore, always avoid these types of soldiers and use his own army. It is better for one to lose with his own army than to win the battle with auxiliary or mercenary soldiers, as you cannot consider any victory won with them as being real.*

It is therefore advisable that you build your own system and effectively manage your resources, so you will not have to solicit help from others who will not hesitate to pull you down when the need arises.

Conclusion

Is there merit in converting the strategies in *The Law of War, The Prince,* and *The Five Spheres* into strategies for political warfare? Absolutely! You may not be able to draw the connections between them at first glance, but you can definitely see that the core essence of these strategies has been practiced in political circles from time immemorial.

There is a common theme behind these strategies, and that is flexibility. If you recall, from my introduction, I mentioned that society has tried to box us into acting according to predetermined structures to maintain some form of civil and fair order. But the reality is quite different. Life is chaos, and only those who are able to adapt to chaotic situations will thrive.

The world is not looking for more "good" people. We would benefit more from having capable people who are not afraid to do all it takes to bring the desired results that we can enjoy. Throughout history, there are stories of good people who, in their fair dealings, only made things worse than they should be.

In the line of battle, if you were to hand over responsibility for your life, would you choose a capable general or a good general? The problem with good people is that they always expect the rest of the world to be good as well. They will not account for the great evil that human beings are capable of.

On the other hand, capable leaders will take all of these into consideration and choose flexible means to deal with each situation according to how they merit. The world would benefit more from more capable leaders, and I hope that with this book, we can begin to work towards creating the movement.

Further Reading

1.   Eudaimonia Classical Knowledge, *The Art of War By Sun Tzu,* accessed April 2020 <https://www.obtaineudaimonia.com/taxonomy/term/200>

2.   Frank James, NPR, *Christine O'Donnell Makes First Amendment Gaffe* 2010, Accessed May 2021 <https://www.npr.org/sections/itsallpolitics/2010/10/19/130671265/christine-o-donnell-stuns-crowd-with-1st-amendment-ignorance>

3.   Gerard Chaliand, *The Art of War in World History: From Antiquity to the Nuclear Age,* The Regents of the University of California 1994.

4.   History (2019), *Watergate Scandal,* accessed May 4, 2021 <https://www.history.com/topics/1970s/watergate>

5.   Ian Chadwick 2017, *The Municipal Machiavelli: Machiavelli's The Prince Rewritten for Municipal Politicians,* accessed April, 2021 <http://ianchadwick.com/machiavelli/>

6.   James MacGregor Burns, *Roosevelt: The Lion and The Fox,* Harcourt Inc., 1956.

7.   John J. Pitney, *The Art of Political Warfare,* University of Oklahoma Press 2000.

8.   Jonathan Powell *The New Machiavelli: How to Wield Power In the Modern World*, Random House Publishing, 2010.

9.   Lawrence Freedman *Strategy: A History,* Oxford University Press, 2013.

10.   Michael A. Ledeen *Machiavelli on Modern Leadership,* St. Martin's Press, 1999.

11.   Michael Edward Mallet, Britannica *Cesare Borgia*, Accessed April 2021 <https://www.britannica.com/biography/Cesare-Borgia>

12.   Michael I. Handel, *Masters of War: Classic Strategic Thought,* Taylor & Francis Book, 1992.

13.   Miyamoto Musashi, *The Five Spheres,* Translated by Ma Trong Tham, 2020.

14.   Niccolò Machiavelli, *The Prince,* Translated by Ma Trong Tham, 2021.

15.   Robert A. Caro, *The Years of Lyndon Johnson: The Path to Power,* Random House Inc., 1982.

16.   Robert Greene, *33 Strategies of War,* Penguin Group, 2006.

17.   Robert R. Leonhard, *The Art of Maneuver: Maneuver-Warfare Theory and Airland Battle,* Presidio Press 1991.

18.   Sun Tzu, *The Law of War,* Translated by Ma Trong Tham, 2020.

www.ingramcontent.com/pod-product-compliance
Lightning Source LLC
Chambersburg PA
CBHW020559270326
41927CB00006B/901